THE STARTUP LEAP

I hope you enjoy reading my book!
Love,
Uttara

THE STARTUP LEAP

FINDING STRUCTURE IN THE CHAOTIC JOURNEY OF STARTUP BUILDING

UTTARA SHEKAR KHEDEKAR

NEW DEGREE PRESS

THE STARTUP LEAP

Finding Structure in The Chaotic Journey of Startup Building

ISBN 978-1-63730-843-1 *Paperback*

     978-1-63730-909-4 *Kindle Ebook*

     978-1-63730-943-8 *Ebook*

*"As you start to walk on the way,
the way appears."*

—RUMI.

CONTENTS

———

To my parents, for checking in on me twice a day
every day for as long as I can remember.

To Gaurav, for being my happy place.

INTRODUCTION

At the risk of sounding like a true millennial, I'll admit: This book is inspired by the *Harry Potter* series. If you are flipping back to the cover of the book to check if you have, indeed, picked up a nonfiction book that claims to explain to you how to build a startup, I understand.

It's true. As a twelve-year-old who was introduced to the world of witchcraft and wizardry by J.K. Rowling, I was immersed in the fascinating universe of magic and of all the things humans could only imagine were true but were not (yet) real. I still remember silently praying on some days for the letter from Hogwarts, desperately hoping the world of magic was real.

Innovative technology is like magic in so many ways because it allows us to create a unique world to the extent of our imagination and sometimes even beyond it. As Clarke's Third Law puts it so aptly, "Any sufficiently advanced technology is indistinguishable from magic."

As I was growing up, I was the tech-savvy kid in my family. I was always experimenting with the different software on our Windows 95 computer. The idea of programming in obscure languages seemed so fascinating to me. Everything about them equated to magic. To me, writing in a unique language that would create things no one had ever seen or experienced was not unlike waving a wand and uttering a spell.

I've spent my entire software career at Amazon and worked with some of the brightest engineers and tech leaders in the world. I've gotten to learn so much from them, and I've grown from being an underconfident programmer to a well-rounded and respected engineer. The company's culture has made me who I am, and I'm very much a through and through Amazonian. I know I can spend my entire career here and continue living this comfortable life.

I'm also a dreamer, and not just in the John Lennon kind of way. I want to use my software skills to create magic of my own. I want to build on my vision of technology and create software that will serve people by helping them in whatever way I can. I know I'm not the only one (get it?).

Today, the world has more technology than ever before. We're slowly but surely becoming more and more connected by the internet. More humans now have access to smart devices. Access to all kinds of information is just a few clicks away. Technology is making its way into every part of our lives—from smart home systems that sit by our couches and can turn on lights and fire up our robot vacuum cleaners to smart wearables that track our sleep and fitness.

It's only growing! Every year, we are in a world that is smarter than the previous one. Large tech corporations have thrived in this economy. According to Statista, by 2023, e-commerce will account for more than $6.5 trillion in sales, representing 22 percent of all global retail sales. According to Research and Markets, the global online education market is projected to become a $319 billion industry by 2025.

The rise of technology is as real now as it was a couple of decades ago. We know with all the technology that has already been built, there's still scope for many more technical advancements to be made. Countless untapped ideas are waiting to be explored in fields like robotics, artificial intelligence, and blockchain. According to Statista, the global market for robots is expected to become a $210 billion industry by 2025. According to another report published by the Organization for Economic Cooperation and Development (OECD), the global annual value of venture capitalist investments in artificial intelligence businesses has grown dramatically, from less than $3 billion in 2012 to about $75 billion in 2020.

As we progress in our careers, we increasingly believe in our capability to build on our ideas and nurture them into successful businesses. But what are ideas when they're not acted upon? They amount to nothing. In my opinion, there are two types of failures: failure from trying and failure from *not* trying.

This book is a step toward bringing people like my colleagues and me the knowledge to materialize our best startup ideas. I want to dive into understanding the process of starting a tech business. I aim to bring structure into the chaos of founding a startup. I want to give tech employees a playbook of sorts, which would enable them to begin the journey of turning some of their unique ideas into actual innovations.

In this book, I talk about the different phases of startup building and the challenges founders face in each phase. I explain how a tech employee can find compelling, fresh ideas and learn how to turn them into successful products by:

- Finding the right customers and learning from them
- Observing the most valuable metrics and trends for their business
- Iteratively working their way toward product/market fit
- Pitching their ideas confidently to investors
- Learning from the unique challenges other founders have faced

Of course, to keep you all engaged, I've generously sprinkled each chapter with many stories from the founders I've interviewed. I've also added interesting, thought-provoking chapters that will help aspiring founders discover how to build to delight, understand why being a purpose-driven business is not just a trend, and learn how to collect unique insights from consumer behavior.

There's more! One of the first thoughts that cross our minds when we think of starting a startup is: Am I ready to make the leap from this comfortable job into a world of unknowns that will have me working long hours with little pay and no work-life balance? This book will also address those apprehensions by giving you a different (and refreshing) perspective on them.

I have interviewed multiple startup founders and researched hundreds of others to create this book. Needless to say, I have learned a lot from each of their unique and eventful founding experiences. I've also attempted to answer the seemingly countless questions first-time founders will undoubtedly have before they even begin on their startup journey.

This book is broken down into four different parts, with each one flowing into the next. The first three parts break down the process of building a startup:

- Part 1—Everything you should know before you begin.
- Part 2—Everything you should build to achieve growth.
- Part 3—Everything you should do to achieve large-scale impact.

Part 4 highlights the catches of being a first-time founder—insights I learned from founders when I asked them, "What is the one thing you wish you had known?" It also teaches you how founders bounce back from the many rejections they face in their journeys.

Tech employees who work in large corporations should be able to pick this book up to understand how to build scalable startups. Founders who are building startups should also be able to pick this book up to learn more about the challenges of the startup phase they are presently in. I hope you find this book valuable enough to become your guide and mentor in your startup journey.

Use this spell-book wisely.

THE STARTUP MINDSET

———

> "It's hard to do a really good job
> on anything you don't think about in
> the shower."

—PAUL GRAHAM, YCOMBINATOR

Saumya dragged himself across the threshold of his swanky Manhattan office on a beautiful summer morning in June. His desk was by the window, overlooking just another busy street in Manhattan. As he settled in with his hot cup of coffee and logged in to his laptop, he sighed.

It was another day of working on business models, another week of convincing his company's high-profile clients to use his recommended business strategies. His work was impeccable. His clients were pleased with his insightful reports and deep analysis. He was getting paid more than he had ever imagined he would. He was in one of the world's wealthiest cities, right in the middle of all the hustle and bustle.

Yet, something didn't feel right.

As he was taking sips from his cup, his head was swirling with many thoughts. *Is this the life I envisioned for myself? How can I do something more fulfilling? Do I see myself climbing this corporate ladder five years from now?* Saumya realized he wanted to do something more meaningful with his time. He was keen on helping people with their finances.

Saumya had been the finance guy for everyone since he was a teenager. His friends consulted him on how and where to invest their money. Even now, his friends from India called him up to understand if their investment strategies were sound. He had a knack for advising people where to put their money, and he absolutely enjoyed it.

Being from a family of businessmen and businesswomen, Saumya had always been inclined to start his own business. He had just been looking for the right idea. Little did he know this thing he identified as merely a hobby was the perfect idea to begin with. That day, something started brewing in Saumya's mind. He realized he would only find satisfaction in his work if he pursued his passion for helping people with their finances.

Within six months, Saumya Shah found himself back in India with a well-researched and detailed plan for his new startup. It would be an online platform for Indians to manage their wealth from anywhere across the country. To resonate with the 1.38 billion people of his country, he named the company Tarrakki, a word that means "prosperity" in the Hindi language.

Today, Tarrakki is three years old and has made investing hassle-free and transparent to millions of Indians. The company serves customers from the largest cities to the smallest towns in India. Tarrakki recently launched Elevo, India's first digital platform for startups and corporations to manage treasuries effectively. It has already processed transactions worth 700 million Indian Rupees ($9.2 million) in its beta launch and aims to process transactions worth five billion Indian Rupees ($66 million) within six months of launch.

How did Saumya manage to quit a cushy job that paid him very well to take on a challenging, new endeavor which was sure to have innumerable unknowns? If I had to give you a single-line answer, I'd say, "Because it resonated with him."

A question every aspiring startup founder will inevitably have is, "Do I have it in me?" This question will come up whenever you start a long-term project in your life. It's a question that comes packed with more profound questions like:
- Am I capable of taking on such a big commitment?
- Will I continue working on it even if I face many hurdles?
- Do I trust myself to stay consistent and persistent?
- Can I do without this comfortable lifestyle?
- Am I ready to face countless rejections?

Before I start addressing some of those questions, the first question I want you to ask yourself is, "Why do I want to start a startup?"

Startups involve a lot of commitment and are full of risks that *you* will have to manage. You will have to convince that cynic in you every day that you are making the right decision by taking this on. You will have to give up, to a large extent, any idea of a work-life balance you had with your regular day job. You will find yourself thinking about your business in the shower, when you go to sleep, and when you walk your dog. You will spend less and less time with your family and friends, and more time in front of your computer, trying to make that sale or trying to fix that annoying bug.

You likely won't be making any real profits for the first two or three years. You will be missing those beautiful strolls at the park with your partner on sunny weekends because you have a long list of things to do that you had to get done yesterday. There will be many customers who do not like your product and do not want to pay for it. Your friends will buy new homes, adopt new pets, travel often, make babies, and it'll feel like everyone else is making progress while you aren't. There will be rejection, frustration, and even tears.

It's no child's play, but every hard thing makes you grow as a person, and building a startup is no different. After knowing everything that has been presented to you so far, here's a question you should ask yourself: "Is this still an itch I want to scratch?"

After having read and watched countless interviews about successful startup founders, I will tell you three qualities that clearly stand out in all of them:
- The ability to relentlessly pursue a perceived goal
- The ability to adapt to changes quickly

- The ability to overcome cynicism

Let's break that down some more, shall we?

THE ABILITY TO RELENTLESSLY PURSUE A PERCEIVED GOAL

Passion is key for building a successful product. The only way you will truly find passion in what you are doing is if the product is relatable to *you*. If it's not something you are interested in, the chances are you will find it challenging to pursue building it relentlessly.

Let me give you an example. I recently had an idea for a startup I thought had high chances to become successful. My friend had been complaining that finding make up artists in Seattle was very difficult. She said she couldn't find a single website that did exactly what she wanted. She wanted to simply enter a few details about the event and the type of makeup she was looking for and have the website give her a list of artists who are available on the selected dates and within her budget. Instead, she had to go through the long process of looking them up on Google, clicking on their websites, filling out lengthy forms, and then waiting for them to get in touch with her via email. It was a frustrating process, and she had to deal with some very clunky user interfaces.

This sparked off the "ideator" in me. I decided to build a website to find and book make up artists with easy to select options, detailed price breakdowns, ratings, reviews, and everything. Since I was committed to writing this book, I decided to ask my husband to build the first version of the website, with a few basic features. He's a software engineer, and this would've been a simple two-week project for him.

Initially, he said he wasn't interested. Still, I tried to convince him by saying the idea could be applied to many other scenarios like booking photographers, cleaners, or drivers. He hesitated for a minute and then agreed. It seemed like he was doing it just for me. He worked on it for about fifteen minutes, then quickly lost interest and started browsing through social media. Now, I know if I'd asked him to build the website for, say, booking personal trainers, he would have been much more interested in it.

You may have seen such examples from your own experiences. When was the last time you worked on something when you were not too keen on it? How would you say the outcome of that turned out? I'm guessing you did not do your best at it.

The relentless pursuit of a goal you are passionate about also lets you be more comfortable with delayed gratification. Building your startup is going to be a grueling journey, and you may only start seeing positive outcomes after the first two or three years. Three years can feel like a long time if you are not genuinely interested in making it work.

THE ABILITY TO ADAPT TO CHANGES QUICKLY

As a founder, you will face countless situations where nothing is going as per your plan. You will expect to make a massive sale out of an expensive marketing campaign, but it may give you disappointing results. Your hypothesis about what your customers will like may turn out to be wrong. You will be expecting to hire that high-performing senior engineer you hoped would become your CTO, but instead, she may choose to go to a big tech company over your startup.

There will be numerous instances where you will be required to make quick decisions and change course until you develop better approaches to accomplish your end goal. You will need to learn to work with the many unknowns by first admitting you do not know it all and then asking the right questions and seeking the right answers.

As a first-time startup founder, another thing to keep in mind while navigating these ever-changing tides is to try not to get too attached to *your solution* for the problem. This is easier said than done, especially if it is something you believe to be core to the product.

Reneta Jenik, the founder of the in-home chef providing app Foodom, found herself in a similar situation when she was first starting out. Reneta built Foodom for busy individuals who wanted to eat healthy, home-cooked food prepared in their kitchen. She came up with the idea because she had personally struggled with finding reasonably priced chefs who would cook in her kitchen. She realized there must be other busy working moms like her who would appreciate having a service like Foodom.

She was very particular about her food being extremely healthy—no sugar, low sodium, and less oil were basic rules in her cookbook. She looked at food as something that helped her stay fit. When she was building Foodom, she wanted the chefs to prepare only very healthy food, like the kind she preferred to eat. She even envisioned the calorie counts from Foodom could be imported directly into other fitness apps. One of her initial customers was her friend, who wanted to book a chef with Foodom to cook for his wife on her birthday. From the menu, he selected minestrone soup, hoping for the traditional, hearty minestrone soup he loved.

He called me a couple of hours later and said, "What is this healthy soup with kale? This isn't soup. This is water with greens! Do you realize not everyone is like you? Some people need normal food!" She laughed as she recalled her conversation with him.

Reneta intended to provide healthy food to her clients but realized not everyone had the same outlook toward food as she does. She was limiting the options for her target market, albeit unintentionally. She quickly changed her course and soon had many positive reviews from happy customers on her website.

Like Reneta, your idea can be perfect for motivating you to build your product, but you will have to let it evolve into the product your customers want. You may have started thinking your idea *will* sell, but when customers tell you what works better for them, you will have to listen to them and adapt quickly.

There will be many more scenarios where founders will need to react quickly and make the most knowledgeable decisions based on the situation. You will find yourself constantly reprioritizing work to get a working but incomplete version of the product out the door just to meet a customer-promised feature delivery date.

Your speed of execution matters. As a startup founder, your aim should be to keep the long-term vision for the product in mind while iteratively building your product by learning from the different internal and external factors to help you mold it better.

THE ABILITY TO OVERCOME CYNICISM

Startup founders may find themselves in situations where they have to continue selling their product to potential customers even when they are aware of statistics that indicate the market is not particularly interested. Failure and rejection are a part of every startup journey, so it is essential to continue being optimistic in the face of such defeats.

If you see yourself as a cynic, you should ask yourself how persistent and optimistic you can be in the face of failures. How easily have you given up in the past when things weren't working out? How much faith do you have in your ability to keep going, as long as you still have resources?

Anukul Veeraraghavan is the cofounder of multiple former startups like Microryza, an online platform for researchers to crowd-fund science projects, and MyUnfold, a former company that aimed to build a new and effective hiring process for employers and interview candidates. Having founded and worked for multiple startups, Anukul realized founders need to have a healthy dose of optimism to keep working on their startups. This often meant believing in their truth to be the only truth, no matter what the market indicated.

> *It's hard to solve these problems. What you really need is a cynical-ish person to be optimistic enough to fix them. It's easy to sit on the sidelines and say, "Don't be cynical," which is what I feel like I'm doing right now. It's much harder to be that person when you're working on a difficult problem. When startups get tough, it gets really tricky for founders. In those times, you need to be a rock. You need to be that person who says, "No matter what, my truth is the only truth. If I say, my startup is worth a couple of million dollars, it is worth a couple of million dollars." You almost want them to be narcissistic to believe it.*

Every founder's journey will have some incredibly challenging moments when they may feel like they are making no progress. Companies like Facebook, which got attention from users almost immediately, are born very rarely. Most founders need to go through the journey of setting up, finding the right team, building on the idea, testing with real users, marketing and selling, measuring progress, and going over the same cycle multiple times to achieve favorable outcomes.

Every step in the process can make you feel like it's not worth the effort. Are you the type of person who ignores the cynic in you and keeps moving?

Now that we've seen the top qualities of startup founders, I must also address the apprehension you may have of leaving behind a comfortable job to build your own business.

In a 2018 Business Insider interview, Mathias Döpfner asked Jeff Bezos what made him go from being an investment banker to a founder. He answered, "When you think about the things you will regret when you're eighty, they're almost always the things you did not do. They're acts of omission. Very rarely are you going to regret something that you did that failed and didn't work or whatever."

If you have dreamed about building your own business someday, Bezos' words likely resonate with you. Would you say you would regret not building your startup when you are eighty?

Saumya Shah had a similar outlook when I asked him what made him leave his high-paying job in Manhattan to move back to India to start a business:

> I know it sounds cliché when people say, "Do you see yourself doing this for the next three years, five years, or ten years?" but I feel like it's true. If I didn't see myself doing this for the next ten years, I would hate myself for quitting my job or leaving New York and coming back to India. I had a pretty set life there.
>
> That level of grit is very important. Like, "No matter what the ups and downs are, I can continue doing this for at least the next ten years." I think that's the most important factor. I saw myself doing it, and that

is what gave me the confidence that if I do this for the next ten years, I'm sure something positive will come out of it.

In Saumya's case, he had to quit his job and move back to his home country to establish his startup in India. You may not need to quit your job immediately. The initial phases of startup building involve coming up with a profitable idea, doing market research, building an initial prototype, and validating the concept with a few initial customers. These are the phases when it is still unclear if the idea will fall flat or take off.

Several founders also choose to put in extra hours every day on their startup until they start seeing some interest and traction from real customers. This way, working on a startup allows them to continue building upon their savings, which they will need once they're working independently.

Another thought experiment to engage yourself in before you make the leap is to ask yourself, "What's the worst that could happen?"

Suppose you quit your comfortable job and decide to start your own business. You may have to keep a check on your expenses more, go out less often, work weekends, and possibly lose some sleep. Even after you do all that, there may still be a chance you fail. But what *is* the worst that could happen?

If you are a high-performing employee in the industry, getting a similar job should be pretty straightforward. In fact, with your startup experience, you may have much more to add to your resumé when you choose to get back into the corporate game.

Let's say you do get to a point in your startup where you've failed. Would that be such a bad thing? Yes, you could have advanced in your career in those few years instead of struggling to set up a business. You will still walk away with some valuable experience about building a startup from scratch, as well as some life lessons about your personality. Those lessons will potentially come in handy when you begin working for someone else. They may make you a better employee because your hands-on experience will essentially help you understand the building blocks of setting up a business a lot better.

So, let me circle back and ask you again: Is this still an itch you want to scratch?

CHAPTER SUMMARY
- Building a startup is going to be an intense journey and may take you a massive amount of energy and time. Every hard thing makes you grow as a person, and building a startup is no different.
- Three qualities that stand out in a majority of the successful startup founders are:
    - The ability to relentlessly pursue a perceived goal: Typically, the founders who have a personal connection toward their idea are the ones who are able to pursue their startup goals relentlessly.
    - The ability to adapt to changes quickly: Startup founders will often need to switch strategies based on

internal or external factors. Founders are expected to adapt to changes quickly without getting overly attached to a single idea or direction.

- The ability to overcome cynicism: In the initial phases, founders may often find themselves in situations where they have to continue selling their product to customers even when the market indicates it is not interested. To keep progressing, it is essential for most founders to have a healthy dose of optimism and to overcome their cynicism quickly.

- You may have hesitations about moving away from your comfortable job to begin a risky, new business. Some ways in which you can appease your apprehensions are by asking yourself:
  - When you are much older, would you look back at your life and regret that you didn't even try to start your own business?
  - If you have a startup idea in your mind, do you see yourself working on it even five or ten years from now?
  - If your startup failed, would that necessarily be a bad thing? You can always prepare for interviews and go back to your old job, but at least you will walk away with some rich experiences and learn some important life lessons about yourself.

THE STARTUP IDEATION

"The value of an idea lies in the using of it."

—THOMAS EDISON, COFOUNDER, GENERAL ELECTRIC

Reneta was in the middle of a busy working day when she first felt a kind of restlessness she had never felt before. She had worked in the industry for twenty years and climbed her way up to the role of marketing director at Intel. Out of the blue, it felt like she was ready for a complete change of scene, away from this familiarity.

She had watched her husband set up his own successful business over the last three years, and something about the prospect of starting out on her own seemed so exciting. There were so many unknowns to be discovered. The risks were high, but it seemed so were the rewards. She found herself thinking of different ideas she could develop on the side to see if it were something she would be interested in, but nothing was clicking.

Then, one day, when she was at work chatting with a colleague, he asked her what she was doing for dinner. Reneta was very particular about feeding her family home-cooked and nutritious meals. After many months of scrounging the internet, she had finally found an affordable chef who had agreed to come over to her house every day to cook the food she approved.

When she mentioned the chef to her colleague, he was stunned. "What?" he exclaimed, "People do that? That's incredible! That would be a great business idea!"

That's when it clicked! In that instant, she just knew what she had to do.

Reneta had a close personal connection with food. Having been sick of eating out many times a week because of not having enough time to cook, she realized she was spending hundreds of dollars each week feeding herself and her family take-out food. She was finding it hard to maintain a healthy weight because much of the food she consumed was not healthy. She and her husband were too busy with work to cook for the entire family every day. She looked at the chef she found as a blessing because her family finally had easy access to healthy, home-cooked meals every day.

As she was thinking more about it, she realized there must be many other families like hers, and that's when she first thought of creating Foodom! Foodom is an online platform that allows residents in a location to book time with local chefs at reasonable prices, who would then purchase the produce, come to their house, and make home-cooked meals for them.

Just like Reneta, for many startup founders, it starts with a hunch. They notice a gap or a trend or identify a single problem they may have solved for themselves but realize many still have. It can feel like a struggle for others who want to build startups but cannot come up with a compelling enough idea. With proper guidance, they can learn where and how to look for the right ideas. This chapter aims to provide that guidance.

At a high-level, this is what you need to keep in mind:
- Find the right market for *you*.
- Identify the gaps that exist in the market.

Let's dive deeper into each of them!

STEP 1: FIND THE RIGHT MARKET FOR YOU

Bill Gross, the founder of the well-known startup incubator Idealab, walked on stage at a TEDx Talk, "The single biggest reason why startups succeed," to talk about the factors that matter the most for a startup's success. He proceeded to explain his research from hundreds of successful and failed startups revealed that while the execution, team, funding, and the idea itself were important factors, the single deterministic factor that stood out was the startup's timing.

> *The results really surprised me. The number one thing was timing. Timing accounted for 42 percent of the difference between success and failure. Team and*

execution came in second, and the actual idea itself came in third. Now, this isn't absolutely definitive. It's not to say the idea isn't important, but it very much surprised me the idea wasn't the most important thing.

Jeff Bezos, the founder of Amazon, said in a 2010 speech at Princeton, "I came across the fact web usage was growing at 2,300 percent per year. I'd never seen or heard of anything that grew that fast, and the idea of building an online bookstore with millions of titles was very exciting to me."

Timing was a huge factor in the success of Amazon because it was started right when the internet was beginning to boom. Similarly, as observed by Bill Gross in the TEDx Talk, the Airbnb founders launched their startup in the middle of a recession when people were looking to make some extra money. Renting out rooms in their homes was an easy way to do so.

A takeaway from these highly successful founders is the timing of a startup is likely to determine whether it will be successful. But how can you find an idea that is right for *you*?

Most founders would say, "Look for problems!" When you find yourself being slowed down or having a clunky experience with something you often use, remember, that could be a problem many like you would be facing. When you talk to your friends or your parents, they could be experiencing some unique problems of their own in their environments. When founders say, "look for problems," they mean to keep your eyes open for opportunities you can grab and solve for millions of potential customers.

I've found this process may not always work. I see people around me face problems all the time. My mother has a problem: due to incompatible versions, she cannot figure out how to make Zoom work on her laptop. I don't live near her, so I am unable to help her out easily. Say I decided to solve her problem by building a solution for customers like her, who require technical experts to help resolve some of their software issues. If I had to build a practical solution, I would imagine creating a network of experts who could visit my customers' homes and solve the problem for them in a cost-effective way. I can see multiple barriers to entry here for me, such as:

- I cannot envision being a customer of the product. Being a software engineer, I can resolve most computer-related issues on my own.
- I am physically in a different location and in a different time zone from the majority of the people I identify as my target customers. It would be difficult for me to confirm my solution is effective.

Some would argue I can resolve such issues by researching more deeply or hiring the right people to do the job. Having multiple barriers to entry would mean I would find the initial stages of my startup building process arduous and potentially expensive. At this point in my startup journey, I would expect a few unknowns, but I wouldn't want to jump head-first into a pool of them.

After researching countless startups and speaking with multiple founders from diverse backgrounds, I have concluded you are likely to find success if your idea stems from:

- A personal connection
- Domain expertise to build an effective solution

In a 2019 Y Combinator video featured on YouTube, "The Biggest Mistakes First-Time Founders Make—Michael Seibel," the cofounder of Twitch and Socialcam, Michael Seibel, believes having a personal connection with the idea is a critical factor in determining the startup's success. A personal connection is what would keep you motivated to keep working on and improving the product. If you can see yourself using the product you are creating, you can envision it from a customer's eyes. This gives you a unique advantage of knowing what your customers want from your product even before building it.

Joon Beh, the cofounder of the online English-language-learning platform Hallo, had a deep personal connection with the problem he solved. When I asked him what inspired him to pursue this idea, he said:

> *I was born and raised in Korea. I moved here to the United States when I was a teenager, so I grew up here, but at the same time, I had to learn new languages growing up. So, a language-learning platform really resonated with me. It was very clear when I came up with the idea because I was the customer who was experiencing the problem.*

Is having a personal connection with the problem enough? It could be, especially if the idea itself drives you enough to find the right resources to build the product. Joon was so excited by his idea it didn't matter to him he did not have the technical skills to build the product:

At my job, I had some interviews with Uber engineers one day, and I was like, "Uber for language learning!" To be honest, the best way to learn any language is by practicing and interacting with real people and immersing yourself in the culture twenty-four seven. In the beginning, I didn't have anything, but I was just so excited I couldn't think of anything else. I decided to build the product.

While having a personal connection to your idea is a great place to begin with, the journey becomes more challenging and more expensive if you have to find reliable resources to build a product for you. If you want the starting phases of your startup to serve as an inexpensive validation of the product, it will get easier if you have some domain expertise.

Arjun Vora, the cofounder of Zira, an online workforce management platform for hourly workers and their employers, used his domain expertise to decide which market to target. Before Arjun decided to build Zira, he worked at Uber as the head of design for the driver app. After talking to many Uber drivers, Arjun realized he was noticing a trend. One of the main reasons drivers preferred to use Uber was because they could adjust their schedules and work flexible hours. They seemed to care about this independence much more than the money they made from their rides.

I eventually went on to lead the driver design team, and my now cofounder went on to lead the Uber for Business team. As part of all these experiences, we spoke to maybe five hundred to one thousand drivers in person across the world. One of the common themes we saw was the drivers weren't necessarily driving for Uber because they made a lot of money. Money was not the incentive. The incentive actually was flexibility. It was like, "I'm my own boss. I can turn on and turn off at any time." For hourly workers, they never had that sense of flexibility and ownership of their own time, which Uber was giving them. So, in spite of the little money they made, they still chose to drive for Uber.

Over many months of such interactions, Arjun realized a similar market existed there for hourly workers. Hourly workers, typically contract workers, are tied to a schedule and do not have enough flexibility to adjust their work hours. Arjun could see the potential of providing all types of hourly workers like chefs, warehouse employees, tailors, nurses, etc., a product that would allow them to walk in and walk out at any time and allow them to create their schedules while also keeping their employers happy.

Arjun envisioned this product could also allow employers to hire a continuous stream of hourly employees around-the-clock. To back up his idea with actual data, he looked online for the market size for the product he was envisioning:

So we started thinking, "How do we bring that flexibility that these gig economy or Uber drivers are getting to the rest of the workforce?" Interestingly, when I looked into these numbers, they were amazing. Seventy to eighty percent of the world's workforce is actually the hourly workforce. The white-collar workforce makes up a very small percent of the workforce. If you see all the apps and the business technology out there, like all the big B2B companies like Salesforce, Workday, Zendesk, AWS, they're all built to improve the lives of the white-collar workforce.

There is very little out there that looks at seventy to eighty percent of the workforce. We started thinking, "How do we make their jobs more flexible? How do we give them a voice in the schedules that their employer sets them? How do we create an upward mobility path for them?" There was very little out there for that. So, because of the specific learnings that we had from these interviews with drivers, as well as this new understanding, and a little bit of the passion we had to help get those hourly workers into that upward mobility path, we decided to build Zira.

By looking up some simple statistics from verified sources, Arjun and his cofounder realized hourly workers comprised a whopping seventy to eighty percent of the global workforce! Arjun and his team used this realization to create an employee management platform, Zira, with a vision to revolutionize the industry by providing the same flexibility and autonomy as Uber drivers to all types of hourly workers.

Identifying a growing trend is usually not too hard if you talk to people about their problems and look up stats about growing industries on the web. When you come up with an idea of your own, search online for facts that verify the market you are targeting is large enough and has some room for improvement. When you have the data to back you up, your confidence in pursuing the idea will grow.

When you come up with an idea compelling enough to turn into a business, you should be able to answer the following:

- I have a personal connection with this product idea because _____.
- I have the right skill set to build this product because _____.
- The _____ market is growing at a rate of ___ percent every year.
- The _____ market is currently worth ___, *or* the ___ market has ___ million potential consumers.

STEP 2: IDENTIFY THE GAPS THAT EXIST IN THE MARKET

At this point, you may have identified a problem space. You may even have started thinking of different ways to solve the problem. Great! Also, remember you are likely not the only person to think of this brilliant idea. There may have been countless other individuals who may have identified the problem and attempted to solve it before you. So, before you get too far into the process, it is essential to identify competing products that exist in the market.

This may not be very straightforward, and simple online searches may not always reveal what you need to know. You will need to dig deeper into existing businesses that solve the same problem, find out how long they have been in the market, learn how their customers receive them, and learn what their customers do not like about them.

Online websites like Crunchbase will allow you to search for new businesses attempting to solve the same problem and give you much information. You may also have to scour through online blogs and websites about new companies solving similar problems in the same industry. As you learn more, note the companies that are likely competitors in the same space.

Once you have a list of your possible competitors, look online for reviews of how they are received. Many companies fail to execute the product well and leave customers feeling unsatisfied with the overall experience. Online ratings and reviews from unbiased sources (that is, not from the company's official website) can be very insightful to understand what your competition may not be doing well. Note down specific details about the different reviews that seem useful for each company you're researching. Don't ignore the good reviews as a lot can be learned from them, too. They will help you understand what customers value the most in the product.

For some founders, the gap isn't always clear. Going back to Arjun's example, when he began building Zira, he realized competing products in the market offered similar features as his own product. One of the biggest lessons he learned in this process was *to not lie to himself about competition:*

> *Definitely do an unbiased validation of the idea. You need to almost detach yourself from the idea to validate it. If you get really attached to the idea, you don't see the truth in the pitfalls. One of the things I did was that I did not see deeply—or I could see it, but I looked away—was the number of competitors that we have in this space. I would come across competitors and think, "Oh, they are not really competitors. They don't think the way we do. We are unique." Don't do that.*

Arjun found himself looking at competition and reasoning the product he's building is unique and offers better features. In retrospect, he says he should have seen the competition for what it is. This is an important lesson to take away from Arjun's startup experience. You may find yourself in a position where you are building a product that is exactly like some of the other products out there, and you may need to dig deeper to understand where the product could improve.

This would involve talking to customers about the existing products and understanding where those products can do better. "Is there really something unique that I'm offering here?" is a question you should be able to answer.

> A lot of times, it's the iteration of the idea that becomes the company as opposed to the idea itself. Don't think of your product as a one-stop shop that will fix everything for your customers. You can choose to become very focused on fixing one single pain point that a major portion of the customers is experiencing.

Iterating over an existing idea but focusing on fixing the most significant pain points has more potential to get you the traction you are looking for to eventually scale up to build that one-stop-shop solution.

You may want to create your startup in a space that is already very popular and has a lot of competition. What can you do in such cases? Saumya Shah, the founder of Tarrakki, the online platform for wealth management in India, realized the fintech market in the US is quite saturated. Seeing there are several wealth management apps in the US, Saumya realized it would be hard to compete in this space in the US. He soon realized the Indian market had a lot of scope for such apps because fintech in India is still largely untapped, and there are at least half a billion Indians who could potentially use an online platform for wealth management in India:

When you're trying to mix finance and tech, there are already hundreds and hundreds of companies in the US in the space. That could be something as simple as Acorns or Betterment or Wealthfront. So, I felt the majority of the gaps, especially in the US market, were addressed. The companies which are addressing those gaps, the products they had, could cater to the Indian market. I was an active user of many of these products, and I felt like there was nothing like this in India.

So, there was the problem statement. There was a gap. Of course, there was a huge demographic of people who were entering this income space, where they have an investable surplus. Some research that goes into it, like, if there isn't a product, why is there no product? If there is a product, is there a target audience? If there is a target audience, why isn't someone else doing it? A lot of companies in India are very well capitalized to set up new ventures. So, why aren't they doing it?

When you look at integration, the focus of traditional Indian financial service players has never been tech. If you take the largest banks in India, they do not focus on tech. So, technology is what was lacking in India. I felt that was the big missing piece. If I could mix tech with a good solution which can address a problem, then I can build something which can scale among the masses.

Saumya knew he wanted to use his passion for helping people with their finances to produce something valuable for them to use. When Saumya saw multiple wealth management apps in the US were flourishing, he realized he could apply a similar solution in a different location, where the gap still existed.

But what if you genuinely had no competition? You may be in a space where your idea is a new innovation that has never been done before. If that is indeed the case, your idea may be well ahead of its time. You may find yourself in this situation if you have already been working closely with cutting-edge technologies the world is still getting used to when you discover an idea you're convinced will be the future.

The decision to create and sell an innovative, cutting-edge product can be a bit of a gamble. It could either become wildly successful or an upward battle to convince the market that they need the product you are selling. The timing of such a product plays a crucial role in this case. If your timing is not right, the market may find the product too ahead of its time and may not yet be ready to receive it. The only way to determine whether the market is ready for your product is by building an initial version of it and testing it out with potential customers.

Jeff Bezos, the founder of Amazon, managed to launch Amazon Web Services (AWS), a cutting-edge cloud computing technology that was truly innovative at the time. AWS had little to no competition when it was launched, and its timing was perfect. Of course, it is important to note Amazon was already a very well-established company when Bezos decided to invest in the cloud computing business, so there was no shortage of funding for the company to build the best product in the market. According to a July 2021 report on Statista, "Amazon Leads $150-Billion Cloud Market," Amazon dominates the cloud computing market by holding a 32 percent share of the market.

Once you have completed your research on the different competing products for your startup idea, create a list of competing products and unique insights about what they are and are not doing well.

At the end of this section, you should be able to answer the following questions:

- The main gaps that exist for the idea I want to build are _____.

- The top three pain points customers who use competing products face are _____.

- The top three things customers value about competing products are _____.

Okay, so you have zeroed in on an idea, looked up your competition, and are aware of the gaps that exist in the market. At this point, you may be able to envision what the ideal product looks like. In this step, one of the biggest mistakes that first-time founders make is they want to build *everything* they've envisioned right from the start. They want to build a product that has the entire end-to-end experience.

The problem with attempting to solve the entire problem in a single iteration is that the scope of the problem becomes too large to tackle. It's *necessary* to narrow down the scope for two main reasons:

- You may end up overwhelmed with the amount of work that needs to be completed before you're ready to show it to actual customers. This, in turn, might dampen your motivation to build even a scrappy version of your product.
- While you may assume you have figured out what customers want with all your research, your assumptions may still be wildly incorrect. So, why waste a lot of time building a product you *think* your customers want when you can spend a little time creating the bare minimum to validate that your customers do like it?

In the next chapter, let's look at different ways to narrow down and hone your idea further so that you can learn how to turn a simple idea into a profitable business.

CHAPTER SUMMARY

- The timing of launching a product is an essential factor in determining its success.
- Startup ideas often start with a hunch. Look for a gap or a trend or identify a single problem you have solved for yourself that many may still have.
- When you look for problems to solve, look within the spaces that are right for you. Your idea will have more chances of succeeding if it stems from:
  - A personal connection to the problem
  - Domain expertise

- Look for statistics from verified sources to find out the size of your target market. Determine if there is a need for a product like yours.
- Identify the gaps in the market by looking through competitive products and doing an unbiased validation of the idea.
- Sometimes, the problem will have many competitive solutions in a single location but may hardly be addressed in a different location. Consider moving to a different but familiar location to build a similar solution for the problem.
- If the product is cutting-edge and you genuinely have no competition, determine if the market is ready for it. Timing is an essential factor. If your product is way ahead of its time, there are chances it may not be adopted easily.

THE STARTUP
BUSINESS MODEL

"Get your facts first. Then you can distort
them as you please."

—MARK TWAIN

In 2007, Patrick and John Collison created, scaled, tested, and
sold a company called Auctomatic for $5 million in about ten
months. They were merely in their teens. Fourteen years later,
it's not surprising they are the founders of Stripe, a startup
that is currently valued at $95 billion!

How did they get there?

Being experienced entrepreneurs at an early age, the two
brothers saw how complex online payment systems were to
operate. They had had a hard time figuring out how to accept
payments for their businesses. They were frustrated with the

amount of knowledge and integration required to set up a company that could accept online payments.

Seeing this was a problem not just for them but also for their friends, the Collison brothers decided to become the infrastructure "middle-men." In less than a year, they had built an online financial platform that would allow any new business to set up its online payment acceptance system in a matter of minutes.

The Collison brothers built Stripe to alleviate a personal problem they had. Being developers who were solving a problem for other developers, they made the product from a developer-first perspective. The interface was so easy to integrate with that many developers still rave about how quickly they could set up their payment systems using Stripe. When they started, they had little idea about how substantial the size of the market was. Over time, as more and more businesses began growing their online presence and required a solution that accepted online payments, their first choice often became Stripe. Today, Stripe is considered a unicorn by its standards. In April 2021, it was valued at close to a whopping $100 Billion in its series H round of funding.

Stripe is the perfect example to showcase founders who built an effective and robust solution to solve their unique problems. I could have used Stripe as an example in my "ideation" chapter, but I think it fits better here because they aced their business model game. Let's find out how.

You can think of a business model as the construction of a beautiful story for your business, where you have a hero (your customer) and a plot. Your hero goes from being dissatisfied and unhappy to being valued and productive by making use of a shiny, new weapon: your product!

This chapter will help you construct your business' story by encouraging you to think of exact answers to *The Six Crucial Questions*. However, the chances are even after you have all the answers, it'll fail. Don't worry, though. Failing is an integral part of the process. With every failure, you'll be testing out a hypothesis, a key piece in your story that doesn't work, and learning how to replace it with a fresh one that will help you make your story more compelling and get your hero closer to a victory.

Rinse, repeat, rinse, repeat, and you'll finally have a business model that will work for you.

You may be tempted to skip this chapter, thinking your business is too small or even nonexistent right now. You are wrong. Even a company that's still in its ideation stage can benefit from a business model. It will help you understand if your business will ever generate profits and is worth putting any resources into.

Helena Ronis, the founder of AllFactors, a web analytics software for businesses to drive marketing and growth, shares the importance of a well-thought-through business model:

> One of the things I always come back to either in my startup or other startups is: What is the business model? I feel like that's something that should be talked about more because, in those fairy tales of

a founder who started this idea and became a billion-dollar company, the fairy tale is always about the idea and not the business model. When you actually look deeply at success stories, you see the founder actually understood the business model pretty early on. They loved the idea and saw the opportunity in the market, but beyond the idea, they also saw how it could be a great business.

To construct your startup story, you will be answering *The Six Crucial Questions* that will help you put your business model together. Open a spreadsheet to get started. We'll dive into specific details in this chapter; you'll want to note them down.

Let's work with a new example in this chapter. Suppose I want to create an online and mobile platform for managing short-term rental homes. Websites like Airbnb and VRBO have become so popular that many customers prefer to stay in them rather than hotels. Consequently, the number of short-term rentals across major cities has shot up. Suppose the owners of secondary homes are too busy to manage these rentals themselves, and I decide to build an online short-term rental management platform. My product will manage bookings for owners across different short-term rental websites like Airbnb and VRBO, use advanced pricing algorithms to determine pricing per night, and take care of cleaning, maintenance, and repair. It will also provide my owners with a simple dashboard where they can see renter bookings, their monthly revenues, maintenance history, and so on.

THE SIX CRUCIAL QUESTIONS
1. WHO ARE MY CUSTOMERS?

Your customers are the people who will buy the product you are selling because it solves a pressing problem in their lives. Open up your spreadsheet and write down a detailed description of who your customers are. Try to be as specific as possible by answering questions like:

- Which age groups do my customers belong to?
- Where are my customers from? Does their location matter?
- What type of professions do my customers have?
- How much do my customers typically earn?
- How do they feel when they face the problem I'm trying to solve? Are they frustrated, bored, or discouraged?
- When do they face the problem?

To know who your customers are, you will need to determine which customer segments represent them perfectly. A customer segment is a section within your target market where the customers have certain similarities. You may have more than one distinct customer segment. Identify each one and list them out. Attempt to be as specific as possible.

If I had to describe my target customer's profile, I would put it down as follows:

- My customers live in North America.
- My customers are typically between twenty-five to fifty years old.
- My customers have a steady income and pay mortgages on their primary and secondary homes.
- My customers typically work forty to sixty hours a week.

- My customers value their time outside of work and prefer to spend it with friends and family.
- My customers are careful about their finances and regularly monitor how their investments are doing.

Remember, it would be easy to mix up some of the descriptions with pseudo-feature requirements like, "My customers would like to view their monthly returns on an online portal at any time of the day." Avoid this tendency and focus purely on who your customers are and what they value.

In some cases, you could have multiple customers. For a company like Airbnb, rental owners and renters are different types of customers they serve using their platform. Similarly, your startup idea may apply to multiple types of customers. If that is the case, note down the profile of your customers within each type in separate lists.

2. HOW CAN I MAKE MY CUSTOMERS HAPPY?

What does your business intend to do to bring value to your customers?

Are you going to be generating extra income for them? Are you going to help them connect easily with their friends or their loved ones? Are you going to entertain them uniquely? Are you going to eliminate their frustration over a problem they often have?

Your product is that crucial weapon in your plot that would allow your hero to become victorious in the end.

Use this section to describe every detail of your envisioned product that would make your customers happy. If your envisioned product does many different things, write them down in the order you plan to work on them, highlighting how each feature would add value to your customers' lives.

For my short-term rental management platform idea, the most significant "weapon" I provide to my customers is it would allow them to save their precious time and rest assured that their rentals are well-managed.

It's important to go into the details in a business model to truly understand how you are adding value. So here goes:

- I make my customers happy by managing short-term rental bookings on multiple short-term rental platforms for them. This saves them a lot of time by not having to manage check-ins or guest requests.
- I make my customers happy by pricing their short-term rentals appropriately such that they make money from them every month. This allows them to be rest assured they receive a good return on their investment.
- I make my customers happy by ensuring proper cleaning is done after a guest checks out from their short-term rentals. This gives them the peace of mind that their property is maintained in good condition.
- I make my customers happy by ensuring any repairs or maintenance that need to be done to their short-term rentals would be managed by me. This allows them not to have to worry about being randomized by maintenance requests every now and then.
- I make my customers happy by providing them with an online interface where they can view their bookings, the

monthly revenue they will earn, the reviews and ratings renters leave about their short-term rentals, and so on. This interface allows them to view all the information they need in one place.

This level of detail allows you to understand if you can address the core values of your customers, which, in turn, will give you insight into whether they will truly find value in buying the product from you.

3. HOW CAN I GET VALUE FROM THE RELATIONSHIP?

Businesses are essentially relationships that need to work both ways. If you provide your customers with many valuable products but cannot get anything substantial in return in the process, you will likely crash and burn very quickly.

Think through the different ways in which your business can make you money. Do you get a cut every time your customers make a purchase? Do you provide your customers with a service they would need to pay for every month? Additionally, it would help to think about how many times your customers would need you. Is this a rare problem for your customers, or would they require your product or service often?

There are many standard business models that largely successful companies use that you can adopt. We'll cover them in more detail later in this chapter. Let me give you a couple of examples of how companies get value from providing their service.

Uber earns by providing a ride-share service where the customer pays the drivers who take them from one place to another, and it takes a cut from each ride. Uber has aced the middleman game of helping customers find drivers easily, which allows them to earn millions of dollars in revenue every year.

Facebook, on the other hand, uses ad sales primarily to make money. They invest heavily in data science teams to create superior customer-engagement algorithms, making customers revisit their different social media platforms. The sheer volume of users on these platforms is enough to get businesses to pay for advertisements on Facebook to get attention from their target customers.

For my short-term rental management company, I would follow the middleman strategy to make money. I will take a cut from each renter who stays in a short-term rental managed by me, let's say, 20 percent. This would be my service fee for giving my customers stress-free management of their short-term rentals.

4. WHAT DOES IT COST ME TO MAKE MY CUSTOMERS HAPPY?

Setting up a tech business can be inexpensive. Keeping track of the things you are spending money on will help you calculate the net profit you make from this business in the long-term. It'll help you decide if the economics make sense for you to continue working with the same idea and features. It'll also help you figure out if you should be looking to reduce costs with cheaper options early on to reduce the money that goes out of your pocket in the initial stages of your business.

The cost to set up and run a business also depends on the type of business you plan to set up. These will include infrastructure costs, operational costs, costs to continue innovating, legal fees, and so on.

For a company like Facebook, costs would include engineering costs to build and maintain the online platform, managing the content and data shown on the platform, and researching and developing expenses to create advanced algorithms to keep users coming back.

On the other hand, for a company like Apple, which sells both hardware and software products, their costs would include engineering costs for software, hardware, and firmware development, costs for patent creation, and costs for manufacturing the hardware, to name a few.

For my short-term rental management business, I would note down my costs as follows:

- Engineering costs to build and maintain the online platform.
- Cleaning service costs.
- Maintenance and repair costs on homes.
- Legal fees to set up contracts with each short-term rental owner.
- Research and development costs to determine competitive pricing.
- Customer service costs.
- Costs to hire managers for in-person inspections.

Note down as many initial setup and recurring costs as you can. You should determine if you have enough capital saved to set up to at least build the most basic version of your product with your own money. To scale up, you may require additional capital from investors. We'll discuss investors in a later chapter.

5. WHAT MAKES ME UNIQUE?

Apart from proving to be an excellent aide to your existing customers, you would also need new customers to seek you out. While word-of-mouth can be very effective if your product gets immediate attention, in this section, you should list down the different things that would make your existing customers rave about your product. In short, what makes your product unique?

Let's take Airbnb, for example. Airbnb provides an excellent platform for verified homeowners and guests, both of whom review and rate each other. They collect reviews from both parties and make ratings and reviews visible to all customers visiting the platform. The transparency of the ratings and reviews is one of the most significant features that makes them unique because it helps owners and guests establish trust with each other.

For my short-term rental management company, this is what I should do to stand out:

- My customers should be able to simply set up their owner contract with me and then have me maintain everything for them, like bookings, cleanings, competitive pricing, and repairs. They should be able to forget I exist while I add money into their bank accounts month over month.
- My customers should be able to see top ratings and outstanding reviews from renters on all the properties I manage for them.

- My customers should be able to contact me at any time during business hours and receive a response with a quick turnaround time.

If I can do all the above, I will be able to keep my customers, my heroes, happy and satisfied with the service I provide to them.

6. HOW CAN I SHOW MY CUSTOMERS I CARE?

A big part of keeping your customers happy is maintaining a healthy relationship with them. You want them to find you reliable, trustworthy, and always available for their assistance.

To maintain a healthy relationship with your customers, you need to enable them to contact you whenever they need your assistance. You can use various mediums like a customer service phone number, a customer service email, a chatbot, or even a social media account to let your customers know you care and are available for them.

A continued healthy relationship with your customers will establish the kind of trust that plays a vital role in the success of a business.

For my short-term rental management business, initially, I would need to ensure I am available during business hours for my rental owners and guests via phone call or email. As I grow my business and start making money, I can consider adding more avenues like chatbots, social media accounts, around-the-clock staff to receive customer service calls, etc.

With this, I wrap up *The Six Crucial Questions* to determine your business model. Let's recap:

- Who are my customers?
- How can I make my customers happy?
- How can I get value from this relationship?
- What does it cost me to make my customers happy?
- What makes me unique?
- How can I show my customers I care?

The primary purpose of *The Six Crucial Questions* is to lay down the entire picture in a structured format for you to look at and potentially brainstorm with your team. Putting everything in one place can help you think through the pieces and bring them together holistically. Such an approach is better than having the different pieces of the picture spread out over sticky notes or, worse, as a swarm of ideas in your head.

Business models are ever-evolving based on new learnings from our internal and external environments. Even successful and well-established companies look to iterate over their business models to achieve more growth.

The one thing to keep in mind while answering *The Six Crucial Questions* for your business is this exercise most necessarily needs to be time-boxed to at most a week. It's very easy to go down the rabbit hole of attempting to get every answer right by doing a lot of research. You must remember it's still a set of hypotheses you will need to validate by actually creating the product. Once you have your initial set of answers, move on to create your very first version to validate your assumptions. We'll cover this in the chapter "The Startup Execution—Phase One."

NAVIGATING THE ENVIRONMENT

As you begin building your business, you will also need to consider external factors as well. Apart from learning if your business idea is likely to grow in the current market, there are a few other questions you should spend time researching:

- If your competitors cannot provide the ideal solution or customer experience, find out why. Is there anything stopping them from doing so that is not in their direct control?

- Are there any specific regulations around the product you are building that you are not aware of?

- Does the product you are building fit with a current trend? If yes, find out if the trend is slowly dying. Will the market be open to receiving yet another product in this space?

- How is the global economy doing? Are people generally optimistic? Are there many new startups coming up? Are investors open to funding new, fresh ideas, or are they taking fewer risks?

If you did the exercises in the "ideation" chapter, you might already have researched the above questions. If you did not, it would make sense to spend some time doing the necessary research. This is another exercise that must be time-boxed. Once you have an initial idea about the market and the different external factors that come into play, you will be able to better determine how your business will do in the current environment.

COMMON BUSINESS MODELS

History is strewn with examples of tried and tested, successful business models, giving countless businesses exponential growth. With the rise of technology, consumers today live very differently from the consumers of the last century. As technology evolves, so do business models. Even today's successful businesses are constantly refining their business strategies to better fit with new generations of technology.

New business models typically use common patterns from previously known and tested business models that have proven to be successful. For example, Uber's founder, Travis Kalanick, is currently using an adaptation of Uber's business model to build his new startup, Cloud Kitchens. Cloud Kitchens is a company that rents out kitchen space to chefs and restaurants so they can produce high-quality delivery-only food to customers. Similarly, Airbnb's model can be applied to any other type of reservation/booking system and does not need to be tied to rental homes.

By studying the common patterns, we can gain much insight into the unique strategies that got successful businesses to where they are. Moreover, there is a possibility these patterns can simply be adapted to fit new business ideas, maybe even yours.

Let's look at seven of the most common business models applied in various successful software-based businesses of today.

MARKETPLACE MODEL

In a marketplace model, consumers use an online platform to get a list of choices for a particular type of product/service they want to purchase. Airbnb and OfferUp are perfect examples for companies that excel in using this model. They offer various choices to their customers with verified, transparent ratings and reviews and provide a secure platform for transactions between buyers and sellers. This model works well because the businesses that adopt it can charge a fee for providing a reliable and robust online platform to their customers.

You can use this business model if your business idea is to provide various choices for a specific type of product or service. Airbnb offers short-term rental stays, and OfferUp offers second-hand goods. If your idea is to connect a buyer of a particular item with many options provided by various sellers, this model will work for you.

MIDDLEMAN MODEL

In a middleman model, businesses provide an easy-to-use and trustable service as a middleman to two sets of customers. The ideal example of a middleman would be Uber, which connects riders with drivers, who have to sign up on the platform as riders or drivers separately. Stripe is another example of a business that plays the role of a middleman.

In the middleman model, many of the service features are built and maintained by the actual business. For example, Uber provides a platform for viewing the distance from point A to point B on a map, decides how pricing would work, shows riders how far away they are from their destination, shows drivers the shortest route to take, and alerts them when new riders are available close to their destination. These algorithms are researched, built, managed, and improved upon by the company to ensure its service is superior as compared to its competitors.

You can use the middleman business model if your business intends to make a specific service more convenient than it currently works. Uber reduced the time required for customers to call for a taxicab by using technology to enable users to click a few buttons to get a car at their doorstep in minutes. Similarly, Stripe offered a payment acceptance technology service to new business owners that allowed them to accept money from buyers in a matter of seconds. These businesses reduced the time required to get some work done by making the interface fast and straightforward.

The middleman model differs from the marketplace model in that the marketplace model offers many selections, each of which is managed by the different sellers. That is, sellers decide how much to offer, the pricing, and what they choose to display. On the other hand, in the middleman model, the transaction typically happens only between one buyer and one seller. The seller, in this case, will have limited options to tweak their preferences and pricing, and do not have much say in how their information is displayed to the buyers.

SUBSCRIPTION MODEL

In a subscription model, businesses provide services to consumers at a subscription rate for a fixed period. The subscription can also be associated with an actual physical product. Consumers typically pay a monthly subscription fee to avail themselves of the service or product. Popular examples of businesses that use the subscription model are Netflix and Peloton.

Subscription models have become popular in today's technology-based businesses. They allow such businesses to provide a growing range of features to justify the monthly subscription fee. This, in turn, enables companies to invest their earnings into researching and analyzing consumer behavior from the data they have collected so they can gradually evolve to achieve higher engagement rates.

Use the subscription model if your business idea is to provide content to your consumers that can keep changing or evolving to better suit consumer needs. The subscription model can be applied to any business that provides content. One of the less explored options here is virtual-reality-based businesses, which can generate fresh content for VR platforms every month.

FREEMIUM MODEL

In a freemium model, a basic version of a service/product is offered free to all consumers, while a subscription fee is charged for consumers who want to access the advanced or premium version. The best example of a business that succeeded in using the freemium model is LinkedIn. LinkedIn created an online platform that was free to be used by job seekers worldwide, but it also provides advanced features in the premium version for recruiters and managers to find top talent for their companies.

The freemium model would work well for businesses that can get a lot of users to sign up for the free account. Other businesses and individuals who want to sell things want to be in spaces that have many potential buyers for their products. So, the chances of making money from this model will be high if the number of users on the platform can scale very quickly.

Use this business model if your business idea has the potential to quickly grow if you offer a free version to users. This business model can also be tricky because you may not always know if your business will reach the scale you assume it would get. So, if you build a free and a paid version for a product that does not get enough consumers for the free version, you may never get enough paying consumers for the product.

HIDDEN REVENUE MODEL

The hidden revenue model can also be called a crowdsourcing model, where the business exists because of the data it collects from its consumers. The "hidden revenue" in such businesses comes from advertising, where buyers of the product are the general public, who are effectively using a free version of the product while being shown advertisements from other businesses that they are likely to click on and make purchases.

Facebook, Instagram, Google, and YouTube are all examples of the hidden revenue model. These businesses are essentially free to be used by regular users but make most of their money from other businesses that want to advertise their products to these users. Needless to say, these businesses are at the top of the technology food chain and are thriving. To ensure other businesses always want to pay for advertisements, they have to continually research how to keep users engaged and return to their platform.

Use the hidden revenue business model if your business has the potential to attract a large number of users you can keep engaged through crowdsourced or in-house content, which you can then use to attract other businesses to advertise on your platform.

RAZOR BLADE MODEL

The razor blade business model came into existence when Gillette realized if they provide consumers with a sturdy and well-functioning razor that lasts a long time, they could offer to produce cheap, high-quality razor blades consumers could then purchase to fit on the razors. This allowed Gillette to generate a massive, repeat customer base for razor blades, which, in turn, generated the business millions of dollars in profits per year.

A technology-based example for the razor blade model is Amazon Kindle. Amazon created a well-designed and long-lasting e-reader called the Kindle, which was similar to the sturdy, high-quality Gillette razors. To use the Kindle, customers have to purchase e-books from Amazon, which can then be read on the Kindle. The massive collection of e-books provided on the platform is similar to the blades provided by Gillette to fit on the razors.

Use the razorblade platform if your business idea is for a product that can help you sell a secondary, cheaper product that requires your customers to purchase the primary product and keep repurchasing the secondary product.

That sums up my chapter on business models. If you've followed along so far and have made notes, you should have a clear picture of the different pieces that will become a part of your successful business startup. If you want to dive deeper into business models, look up Alexander Osterwalder's business model canvas online. Osterwalder provides a strategic template for constructing new business models using nine "building blocks." His model is widely used in the industry for creating new business models.

CHAPTER SUMMARY

- Creating a business model for your startup is essential to understand the deeper, moving pieces of the business that will help you determine whether the business will be profitable in the long run.
- Use *The Six Crucial Questions* to determine your business model:
    - Who are my customers?
    - How can I make my customers happy?
    - How can I get value from this relationship?
    - What does it cost me to make my customers happy?
    - What makes me unique?
    - How can I show my customers I care?

- Consider external factors that may impact your business. Are there any regulations or laws that prohibit you from running your business a certain way? Are there any natural calamities or pandemics that can affect your sales? Research, review, and brainstorm these factors with your team.

- You can adopt common patterns from existing business models that a lot of successful businesses use. Some of them are:
  - Marketplace model
  - Middleman model
  - Subscription model
  - Freemium model
  - Hidden revenue model
  - Razor blade model

THE STARTUP COFOUNDER

"You need someone that behaves like James Bond more than you need someone that is an expert in some particular domain."

—SAM ALTMAN, COFOUNDER OF Y COMBINATOR

Ashish sprung out of bed that fateful morning. He and his cofounder were going to meet a promising venture capitalist to finalize their very first round of funding. He was optimistic and looking forward to locking in the deal to begin working on the next phase of their startup. Little did he know he was in for a surprise.

The two of them had built their startup from scratch and had only recently started seeing customer traction. Their partnership had been strong so far, and the future of their company looked promising. Even though they were operating as a legal company, this was the first time they were going to sign legal papers signifying their partnership before closing the deal on the funding round. Their informal partnership had just worked so far, and since they considered themselves a small tech business, there had been no need to create legal documents.

With much eagerness, Ashish began mentally preparing for his meeting with the venture capitalists. He felt recharged and confident about closing the deal. He walked into the office where the meeting was to be held and met his cofounder enthusiastically. A few minutes into the conversation, his face fell. His cofounder had been nervously waiting for Ashish to arrive; he had some news he wanted to break to him before the meeting.

"I think I should get a higher equity because it was my idea," he suggested. Ashish was dumbfounded. This news had come as a complete surprise to him. He had to take a moment to register what he had heard. As the realization settled in, he began to get angry. He felt betrayed and cheated. In that instant, he lost trust in his partner completely.

The timing of the news was terrible! They were just a few minutes away from walking into a room to meet their potential investors.

His first gut reaction was to try to convince his partner they had built their startup together from the ground up. The idea hardly mattered without the execution. When his partner wasn't ready to understand, he immediately began to regret that he did not have any official documents stating their equal partnership.

To Ashish, coming up with the idea was something that took place much before the first block had been laid in the startup building process. Moreover, his partner had not done any extra research or analysis before approaching Ashish with the idea. They had worked together—figuring out their target customer base and market size by iteratively building upon the product. He believed he had genuinely worked with as much commitment and passion toward the startup as his cofounder, right from the beginning. He wanted an equal share of the pie but was now beginning to question if he even wanted to continue building this business with his cofounder.

When they finally went into the meeting, it was clear to the investors they needed to work on their partnership. Needless to say, they did not get the investment.

This was the story of Ashish Rohil, the cofounder of former company madbooks.com, a website that sold second-hand books online to customers in India. No prizes for guessing why madbooks.com is not a surviving company today.

Several of the founders I interviewed for my book highlighted their experiences with cofounder relationships that did not work out.

Nikhil Aitharaju is the founder of multiple Silicon Valley startups like Topic, an AI content optimization platform that helps marketers create high-quality content at scale, and TINT, a visual user-generated content marketing platform. In my interview with him, Nikhil highlighted the importance of a good cofounder relationship by relating it to a marriage. According to him, finding the right cofounder is no different from finding the right person to marry. After all, a startup has the potential to run for at least ten years, if not more, and the cofounders make many significant decisions in these initial crucial years.

> *It's like picking your life partner for when you're marrying someone. You need to pick the right person who can build this house with you. [It is the] same with startups. You need to pick the right cofounder—whom you trust and who can help you execute that vision or who can execute that vision for you. So, I think picking the right cofounder is very important.*

> *Working with really close friends could be a good idea as long as you know you trust the person. I met my cofounder randomly, like I didn't even know him, but we hit it off because of our personalities. So, maybe trying to work together for a couple of months would be good, but be transparent about it like, "Hey, let's try this out, and we'll see if we really like our working style." If you're able to build on this relationship like you're dating for a couple of months and being truly transparent, that is something I would recommend.*

Founders often find themselves arguing, brainstorming, and likely even spending more time with their cofounders than they do with their spouses. However, there's a critical difference between the two relationships. With spouses, your goal is to nurture a relationship that is mainly pleasant and agreeable. You may have your fair share of arguments, but it would be in both of your best interests to sort out issues so you can live peacefully around each other. You're building toward each other's long-term happiness.

On the other hand, in a cofounder relationship, your goal is to build a successful business. You want to look for a cofounder you enjoy brainstorming with. Intellectual arguments with strong opinions from all parties are healthy, even encouraged, as long as they develop an ideal path forward for your product. You should also be able to disagree with each other respectfully and commit entirely to the final decision.

Think of your relationship with your cofounder as that of a colleague from work whom you enjoy brainstorming with, and over time you have grown to like each other and have become great friends. Similarly, with your cofounders, you should be able to work long and grueling hours together to tackle challenges, celebrate the most minor successes, and most importantly, be vulnerable enough to express openly to each other.

Even after you have found a great set of cofounders who are as committed to the product as you are, there may still be times when you will find yourself arguing over decisions and priorities for the future of your product for days at a time. Oftentimes, this nerve-racking decision-making process can be simply turned into a numbers game.

Aditya Sharma, the cofounder of Souled Store, an online merchandise and fashion retail store in India, explains how that worked for him. His company makes t-shirts with cool designs, the operative word being cool. Since "cool" can be highly subjective, he and his team found they often debated on which idea seemed cooler. It took Aditya and his cofounders a few heated arguments to realize there was a simple way to resolve such problems—by voting!

Every time a fresh batch of t-shirt design ideas had to be short-listed, they decided to vote on it as a team. Since they were four cofounders, this would sometimes end up being an even number. When that happened, they involved more members of the team, like the other nonfounding members. They realized deciding based on numbers was much more manageable and produced less conflict than convincing others of why their opinion is more valid than others.

Debating on which design idea is better is just one aspect of your relationship with your cofounder. One of the key mistakes new founders make while looking for a cofounder is that someone agreeing to do the work will commit to the role with as much passion as themselves. This may not always be true.

If you believe you have found someone who would be the ideal cofounder for your startup, you want to make sure that person is as committed and passionate about building the product as you. If you find yourself being approached by a friend to build a startup together, you should also assess whether you are interested in the idea. While an immediate personal connection for the problem may not always be present for a new cofounder, the cofounder must see themselves as someone who could nurture a deeper personal connection for the product over time.

In other words, if my husband were building an app related to fantasy football and asked me to be his cofounder, I would pass on that offer because I simply do not see myself having a personal connection with fantasy football. On the other hand, if he was creating an app to, say, help people reduce their carbon footprint, I'll consider it a lot more seriously because I can see myself cultivating a personal connection for a sustainability-based product even though I may not be actively thinking about it now.

Na'ama Moran, the cofounder of restaurant food supply business Cheetah, found herself in a similar situation before building one of her former startups. A friend of Na'ama's from school approached her to start a new business to help other small businesses get more digitized. At the time, Na'ama knew she wanted to run her own business and was looking for the right idea. This is what she had to say about her experience becoming a cofounder:

> *First, there has to be an inspiration—something you feel compelled to do. Then you have to come to pass this through the rigorous sieve of the market research, but the inspiration has to come first. In this case, it was my cofounder who came up with the inspiration. As we started working together, I connected to the inspiration, which was about helping small businesses in a world that is getting increasingly digitized. So, I would say sometimes the inspiration comes from you, and sometimes it comes from your cofounder. But you have to be connected on the same level.*

Let's go back to the most basic question about cofounders.

DO YOU NEED A COFOUNDER?

A startup founder generally begins with the mindset of building an outstanding product that everyone will love. While this mindset is ideal for getting excited about building the business, the journey of actually building the product can be quite lonely.

Even if you have the expertise to build a product, *you* alone may not always know if your product is the right one for your customers. You will need to have healthy brainstorming sessions with a group of trusted individuals who are unafraid to question your opinions, beliefs, and hypotheses to help you feel confident your business will fly.

If you have a network of people with relevant expertise who are happy to engage with you in multiple brainstorming sessions and discuss ideas and features with you, you may be able to build the product by yourself as a solo founder. You will need to create a healthy network of mentors and subject matter experts who can guide you in building your startup.

Reneta Jevik is a founder who decided to go solo after being in a bad cofounder relationship. Reneta is the founder of Foodom, an online platform that allows customers to book time with chefs, who would then come over to cook fresh and nutritious food for them at reasonable rates. When Reneta began working on Foodom, she had an ex-colleague from work which took on the role as the CTO and a founding member. At the time, Reneta agreed to work with him because he expressed interest in the product and also wanted to start a business.

As they continued to build, the relationship between the two founders turned sour. Reneta felt like her CTO wanted more of a say in the CEO-type of decisions in the company, and this left her feeling helpless. Moreover, these issues coming up at such an early stage of her company was the last thing she wanted to deal with. She decided the best course of action would be to end the partnership and to start over on her own. Reneta is one of those solo founders who has built herself a rich network of mentors and technical experts to advise her on the road she wants to take.

On the other hand, if you are the only person who is actively thinking about the scope of the product and do not have a network to help you out, you may miss out on some useful insights of having more than one mind working toward strategizing for the success of your business.

You may also find most of your friends and family still work at their regular day jobs and do not relate to the challenges and struggles of building a business from the ground up. Even if they do express interest in helping you, if the product or service is not something they are personally invested in, it would be quite hard to have them engaged with you for the entire startup journey.

When we look at the history of the most successful companies today, most started out with at least two founders. According to a Y Combinator article, "How to Find the Right Co-Founder," by Harj Taggar:

> *If you look at a list of the most successful startups in history, think of Apple, Facebook, Google, Microsoft.*

They all had cofounders when they started. And now I think sometimes people forget this point. Because when you think of these great iconic companies, you associate them with a single person, usually the CEO, who over time rose to become prominent, famous, and a bit of celebrity. You know, when you think of Apple, you think of Steve Jobs, when you think of Microsoft, Bill Gates, and when you think of Facebook, Mark Zuckerberg, right?

I think it's completely true that over time, and we're talking at this point decades because that's how long successful startups are around for. Over that time period, it's pretty common for one person to kind of really drive the company, become the figurehead for it, and stick out that company for a long period of time. And that's why we remember those people.

But we're talking about the earliest stages of starting a company. And in those days, all these founders had cofounders they leaned on for all the reasons I just mentioned. So, I think it's always important to remember when you're starting a company and wondering whether you should have a cofounder or not."

To illustrate the importance of working with cofounders more, let me give you an example. Suppose you are an engineer who is handed a big project at work where you are responsible for designing and building a prominent feature for the overall product. In a big tech company, you will begin by looking at the available technical frameworks and technologies that would work well for this feature. You will then read through existing designs that have been used to build similar features successfully. You will then develop a design document that highlights the best strategies for building your feature, why they are the best, and the recommended strategy's execution phases.

This document is then reviewed by a group of people with expertise in the domain who can help you decide if the recommendation is the best path forward. The review of the document is one of the most important phases in the development of the feature. It gives the team confidence about the execution plan. Since many minds were involved in the creation and approval of the design, there is a greater chance the risks, points of failure, and false presumptions are thoroughly vetted through this process.

However, an engineer who architects, designs, and builds a feature all by herself may not be able to understand the presumptions she's making, or see the nuanced flaws in her design, or be aware of the new technologies she hasn't heard of.

Similarly, as a solo founder, you may be able to do a lot of research and talk to many customers, but it's still primarily your perspective at the end of the day. Even if you hired a team of engineers and advisors to work with you, depending on their expertise, you may or may not get them to think critically about the product, feature, or strategy.

If you decide to be a solo founder, do remember the likelihood of burning out due to the sheer variety of tasks is much higher. You will need to manage the executive decisions, the execution, as well as the operational tasks—from designing the right product, finding and engaging with customers, managing finances, creating your business plan, marketing your product, pitching to investors, and the list goes on. If you do not have enough capital initially to hire employees to take on some of this load, the chances are you will spend your time filling into each one of those roles yourself.

Depending on your personality, it may be a pragmatic decision to build a team of trusted and passionate cofounders with who you get along with who will agree to build your product with you. That being said, if you want to find cofounders, you should learn how to select the right ones for your business.

HOW CAN YOU FIND THE RIGHT COFOUNDER?

Some startup founders begin with an idea and find a group of friends who are willing and passionate about building the startup with them. If you are one of these people, you're incredibly lucky! When you work with well-known people and with whom you can have open conversations, you do not need to worry about building a rapport with them. In this case, you will only need to ensure you have varied skill sets, and each one of you has a significant role to play as a founding member.

Aditya Sharma, the cofounder of the popular pop culture and fashion apparel brand from India, The Souled Store, found his cofounders by simply discussing his startup idea with some colleagues from work:

> It honestly wasn't well thought through. It wasn't even a serious discussion in which I had the intention of

getting them on board. It was more like, "Hey, here's an idea, let's get together and do it." Luckily for us, all of us did have different skill sets. So that worked out really well.

Clearly, for Aditya and his cofounders, a successful business was in their stars. Not everyone's journey will be as straightforward as Aditya's. If you don't have a set of friends who want to build a startup with you, you'll need to go through the process of finding and evaluating potential cofounders.

Begin by tapping into your network to see if you can find a friend or a colleague you enjoy working with and have intellectually stimulating conversations with. If you know someone smarter than you and you believe they would make a great partner, engage them in a conversation and see if they will be willing to build a business with you. Finding a cofounder like this is a process of trial and error. Sometimes it works out, and sometimes it doesn't. When it doesn't, you may have to go back to square one and start looking again. Unsurprisingly, the widely accepted term for this is "cofounder dating."

If you do not have the skillset to build the product you envision, you should look for cofounders with the required skill set. Say you are a Product Manager in the tech industry, and your startup idea is to build a software product. Even if you have the best ideas for your product, you will still need someone with the technical skillset to execute those ideas.

However, this does not necessarily mean you cannot validate the idea without a technical cofounder. You can find freelance developers on the internet who can build you a scrappy proof of concept. Arjun Vora and his cofounder, the founders of the workforce management platform for hourly workers, Zira, were product designers at Uber when they decided to work on the startup together. They were considered a "dream team" and had even earned a reputation as "intrapreneurs" by many within Uber, as they would innovate and build new products for the company. It was only natural to take that kind of a working relationship and turn it into a cofounder relationship.

When Arjun and his cofounder first got together to build Zira, they began by doing market research and designing the core concept for the product. They got freelance programmers from India to build a very basic version of the prototype at an affordable price. They then used the prototype to get initial feedback from potential customers like restaurant owners and local store managers. This approach enabled them to confirm there is a sizable market out there for their envisioned product. With these initial experiments, they soon realized their concept and idea were really coming together. The first signs of traction helped them commit to the product and work toward building a bigger technical team to build the actual product for them.

On the other hand, if you are a software engineer looking to build a software-based business, you likely have all the technical skills to create the product. You would be surprised at how many nontechnical skill sets are required for growing a software business. When you're on a hunt for a cofounder, you should keep in mind the product goes beyond just the code or even the initial idea. Customer engagement, market research, financial management, pitching to investors, and product marketing are all essential skills a software engineer may not be particularly good at.

As an engineer, you may be tempted to build on your startup idea and worry about the "business-y" aspects later when you're still working on your idea as a side project or a hobby. This approach may work if you commit to finding people with complementary skill sets early enough in the process. You may even want to time-box your prototyping phase so you do not spend an extensive amount of time building something not many people will be interested in.

Apart from finding someone who has complementary skills, you want to make sure you get along with your cofounder, especially in situations that can get stressful or demotivating. Suppose you have found a friend or a relative who wants to start a business and is passionate about building a startup with you. If you have only been around this person in stress-free situations, when both of you were relaxed, you will not have an idea about how this individual responds to stress. Do they panic? Do they feel so dejected when they see a customer reject them that they do not want to continue working on the idea? Do they promise to deliver more than they actually can before a strict deadline?

You also want to look for cofounders who wish the same outcomes from the startup experience. Are you creating a business for the sole purpose of making money? Or do you care more about helping people? Do you value quality over quantity? Do you prefer to move fast and break things, or move slowly and steadily? Find out if your potential cofounder wants similar outcomes.

Another critical factor is determining whether you and your cofounder can get on the same page about values. What type of company culture do you want to build? What would the core values of your company be? What is your take on creating ethical relationships with vendors, customers, and employees? With how much integrity do you want to build this company? Having open conversations about these topics will help you decide if you and your prospective cofounder can get on the same page and build toward a single vision for the company.

Arjun Sundararajan, the cofounder of Zync, an interactive online platform for running engaging virtual events, explains the various questions founders must ask each other to ensure they will be aligned when it comes to making important decisions for their startup:

> *In my first startup, by the time we were one and a half to two years in, it was starting to become really hard to stay aligned and pulling in the same direction, mostly because we all had very different ways of doing things. This happens when you're doing it for the first time. So, we had no idea about it when we were going in. We didn't even know what kind of questions to ask each other to see whether this was actually a good fit. It's like going on a first date and then saying, "Let's do this," which is not ideal.*

Instead, we should have asked questions like, "What do you think should be a potential exit for this company? Do you think this should be a venture-backed business as opposed to a lifestyle business?" and so on. For all these questions, we didn't really have an idea of each other's opinions, and not knowing that is sort of a recipe for disaster.

So, in my case, once we raised about $1.2 million or so, we spent about six months trying to find product/market fit in one direction. Then our runway started to get shorter and shorter, but we were spending more than 50 percent of our time aligning than actually doing the work. That's expensive; you really don't want to do that.

There are also some personality traits you want to look out for when committing to building with someone. No matter how interested or committed this person is to the idea, if they make you feel stressed or dejected because of their skepticism, you will have a hard time making the relationship work.

Your aim should be to find a cofounder who works so well with you that you can focus entirely on just building the startup. If you find yourself thinking more about how your cofounder will react or whether they have the same standards as you do, then the relationship is not working toward the success of your startup.

To evaluate whether a person will be a good fit as a cofounder, you will need to spend some time working with them. Let this person know that you want to see how well you both work together and how your responsibilities are split up, and work toward making progress on a particular goal within a set amount of time, like two months.

In my opinion, two to three months of working together with a potential cofounder will give you enough time to evaluate each other and decide if you want to move ahead with the partnership. It's essential to keep in mind you do not want to spend more time than you had allocated for this process. Remember, finding a cofounder is very much like dating, where you may need to repeat this process multiple times until you've found someone who is compatible.

Now that we've discussed finding the right cofounder, let's move on to the final question.

WHAT SHOULD YOU DO AFTER YOU HAVE FOUND A COFOUNDER?

Once you have found a cofounder whom you trust and have a great working relationship, you can move on to establishing the relationship in a formal, legal contract. Cofounder relationships turn sour more often than you can imagine, so find a good lawyer to legalize the agreement as soon as you have decided to work with each other to build the product.

This agreement, called a founders' agreement, includes the necessary details to ensure the business can run smoothly. According to an article by Shikhar Ghosh and Marilyn Morgan Westner in the Harvard Business School Accelerate, "Key Terms to Include in a Founders' Agreement," the agreement should include four key areas, in which you will:

- Decide on the titles, roles, and responsibilities of each founder.
- Describe the decision-making rights to ensure founders do not step on each other's toes when it comes to making important decisions for the company.
- List down what each founder brings to the table, such as intellectual property, initial capital, and time invested.
- Decide on the equity split and vesting schedule for each founder, along with any contingencies in case any unexpected situations arise while running the business.

Before creating your founders' agreement, have an open conversation with all the founding members to decide on the company's titles, roles, responsibilities, and equity split. If there are multiple founders, more than one person may want to hold the title of CEO. In many cases, the CEO becomes the company's face, so remember a primary quality CEOs must have is the ability to convince and sell effectively. They must have the capability to tell a great story and inspire the people around them. If a founding team member portrays the qualities of being an influential leader, it would be ideal for them to take on the role of the CEO.

Another point of contention that must be discussed by the founders beforehand is to decide how to split the equity. If your startup is still in its early stages where none of the founders have accomplished much, the recommendation from business advisors would be to go with an equal split. This is because an unequal split may result in unnecessary politics and division among the founding members, which may, in turn, divert your attention from focusing on building your business and making an impact.

If, on the other hand, you have spent a lot of time researching and building your startup and have made enough progress to see initial interest from customers, or you are contributing a majority of the initial capital to help build the business, you may feel you deserve a larger share in the equity. In such cases, have an open discussion with your cofounders about an unequal split and see how they respond to it. Your aim should be to ensure all the founding members are satisfied with the compensation they will receive from the contract. They should feel incentivized and motivated to continue putting in their efforts into building a successful startup.

It may feel awkward to sign a legal contract with your cofounders, especially if they are friends or relatives. Many people are not inclined to bring the formality of a paper trail into their relationships. As cofounders, it is important to speak openly with each other about any requests, wants, or hesitations. Establishing clear boundaries regarding roles, responsibilities, and work to be contributed in a legal document is a step in that direction. So, while it may be uncomfortable to bring up legal contracts in such cases, having them in place will allow you to continue to maintain a clean and healthy relationship with each other.

Now that you have a good idea of looking for compatible cofounders, let's look at how you can begin executing your startup idea.

CHAPTER SUMMARY
- Evaluate if you need a cofounder by answering the following questions with honesty:

- Are you the sort of person who works better independently than with other people?
- Do you have the expertise, advisors, and network to build the startup by yourself?
- Are you self-motivated, or do you often feel dejected by failures or hurdles in your journey?
- How do you perform under stress?

- If you choose to find a cofounder, here are some of the questions you should answer during the evaluation process:
  - Does your potential cofounder have complementary skill sets?
  - Do you and your potential cofounder get along with each other?
  - How does your potential cofounder react to stress?
  - How does your potential cofounder handle situations where you are stressed?
  - Do you and your cofounder have common values? Can you build toward a single vision for your company?
  - Are you able to engage your potential cofounder in brainstorming sessions about the product?
  - How does the relationship with your cofounder make you feel?

- Once you have found the right cofounder:
  - Prioritize having open discussions about the contributions of each founder and the consequent rewards they should receive from the startup.
  - Discuss titles, roles, and responsibilities of each founder.

- Decide equity split, initial contributions like intellectual property and capital investments, and vesting schedules.
- Find a lawyer to legalize the relationship in a founders' agreement.

THE STARTUP EXECUTION—PHASE ONE

———

"If you are not embarrassed by the first version of your product, you've launched too late."

—REID HOFFMAN, COFOUNDER OF LINKEDIN

"Don't overthink it, just build it. Once you build it, people will come," said Anirudh Sharma, one of the most unconventional founders I interviewed for my book. Anirudh is an MIT Media Labs graduate and the inventor of two ingenious innovations—LeChal and Air-Ink.

LeChal, an expression in Hindi that means "take me along," is a smart shoe primarily created to guide the visually challenged. It provides haptic feedback using the sense of touch and ties that technology to a GPS service. This innovation enables the shoes to vibrate in the direction the person wearing them should move.

Air-Ink, as you may have guessed, is ink produced from the air. By that I mean—from air pollution! Today, Air-Ink is used by artists and celebrities from around the world to promote sustainability. In an April 2021 article on *Vogue*, "The Printing Ink on Naomi Campbell's Pangaia Sweatshirt Was Made From Air Pollution," the well-known British model and actress Naomi Campbell wore recycled and organic cotton sweatshirts and sweatpants from Pangaia, and the prints on them were created using Air-Ink.

Needless to say, Anirudh's innovations were much-lauded and praised for their high social impact at a global level. How did Anirudh turn his out-of-the-box, innovative ideas into actual products produced at scale and sold by his businesses?

> *In the early stages—when you have an idea—you will have doubts. That is the most exciting phase because when you have an idea, it's just an idea in your head. So, in the early stages, you should focus on testing your hypothesis. You can quickly assemble a prototype and talk to friends who are good at other things. For example, if you do not know how to hack a printer, talk to a person who's an expert in electronics. Bring them in and say, "We can pay you. Let's modify the printer, and let's make it do something different."*
>
> *I would say the early stages are very, very important... in a way that you can quickly move from an idea in*

your head to a prototype that can speak for itself. So,
don't overthink it, just build it. That's the crux of it.

As Anirudh explained how he used pollution from cars and
fed it into a "hacked" printer to validate his hypothesis for
Air-Ink, he shared his approach toward any type of innovation—focus on your phase one and work toward testing
your hypothesis.

Phase one of startup building can be similar to that long,
trippy rollercoaster ride where the highs are exhilarating
and the lows nerve-racking. This phase can be considered the
experimental stage of your startup, where you are learning
and unlearning, testing, measuring, and iteratively building
the most consumer-friendly version of your product. In this
phase, you will gradually begin to materialize your startup
vision into an actual product. While this may sound intimidating, it most likely looks like sitting at your desk in your
pajamas, trying to get some code to work.

Even after you have reached this phase, you do not necessarily
have to quit your regular job. A realistic way to pursue your
startup dream would be to spend your nonworking hours
building a prototype for a product that you can validate.

Leighton Healey, a serial founder from Canada who has
cofounded tech startups like KnowHow, a product that provides dispersed teams with instant access to a company's processes and "how-to" workflows, and Bootkik, an AI-driven
platform for sharing step-by-step expertise with others,
describes the process of transitioning from an employee to
a founder by using the concept of on-ramps and off-ramps.

Leighton believes starting a business should be a gradual process, similar to how you get on a ramp to merge onto a freeway:

> First, I would say founders should understand what I believe is the concept of on-ramps and off-ramps, just like merging onto a freeway. What I mean by that is: jumping into a new venture rarely means you stop everything else and start something new. People call it a side-hustle because there's a lot of value in actually starting something at the corner of your desk.
>
> Very rarely, what you think is going to be a great idea is actually going to be a great idea. You also have to go through this process of learning through the years. The market doesn't care how smart you think you are. The reality is people will pay for solutions that solve real pressing pain points in their life. If you can't learn to really serve customers and learn how to listen, you're going to fail.
>
> I just find a lot of the characteristics that cause a person to have the confidence to leap sometimes have the same characteristics that make it difficult for them to be a good listener. To be someone who genuinely has the ability to lower themselves to that front-desk person in a hotel, you need the ability to take on that service orientation.
>
> Oftentimes, it's a big flip because you go from someone who has a reputation and a title and a business card with a logo that's really respected to now, on

the ladder of importance, you're just below that guy
replacing that light bulb in the hallway. That ability to
recorrelate yourself in the constellation of priorities is
difficult. For a lot of people, their pride and ego really
send them back to the big cushy job.

First-time founders who can find the confidence to begin their own startup may have once been employees working in comfortable jobs where they had a good reputation and were highly respected. When they take off their employee hat and put on their founder hat, they should keep in mind their importance drops with that transition, from someone much respected to someone largely unknown who needs to work their way up the ladder once again.

Your customers don't care enough about your product yet to give you the same kind of respect that you got at your tech job. Even the employees you hire may not be the cream of the crop as you may only have enough budget to hire the less skilled, junior engineers to do the work for you. Your exposure to colleagues who are much smarter than you may become limited. In the initial phases, you will need to make peace with these kinds of changes and learn how to navigate through them with some level of comfort. Leighton also had some insightful suggestions for people who have made the decision to start a business:

> *Once a person has really resolved to make the startup*
> *happen, I would encourage them to do three prelim-*
> *inary activities.*

First, I would begin to cut my personal life burn by 50 percent immediately. I would start by saving half of my income every month. I would ideally give myself a six- to twelve-month cushion. One of the things that are difficult once you make that leap is you don't realize your lifestyle is going to take a huge hit, and that proverbial well that comes every few weeks is not going to get topped up again.

Second, I would take a step back and say, "Which are the relationships I want to shore up right now when I have influence and the ability to leverage my role and my title, which will serve me well once I leave?"

Third, is to make peace with any enemies I've made—competitors in my field whom I have some silly school ground rivalry with. You never know, when you're out on your own, who you're going to need. To have as many friends as possible serves you well.

Now, you have your priorities with work. You have to deliver those so you leave the door open. This is not one of those scenarios where you want to burn the ships. You don't want to march out naked, you know? At the end of the day, that's really not how you do it because the business you left very often becomes your first customer.

When you're in the process of transitioning, most people don't break up well with their company. Their way of processing the fact they're leaving is they just bash the company. They talk about the things that are wrong with it and how they would be so much better on their own. For some others, they start to get nostalgic and talk about the company like they're dying. That creates a weird aftertaste in your colleagues' mouths. The best thing you can leave your colleagues with, in my opinion, is you are a high performer who did what you said you were going to do. You were a great friend, and they just can't imagine you not being part of the team. So, when you do leave, the reality is you have a great source of future hires, which are the people who you left with a positive taste in their mouth.

There's a lot to learn from Leighton on how to leave things with your colleagues and your company when you're about to make the transition. Ensure you are in a good position to quit your job when you're ready to make the leap by saving up sufficient funds, building up your network, and making peace with any enemies you may have made in the past. You want to be on good terms with everyone when you leave your company because you never know when you will need those connections. Ideally, you want to quit your job after validating a market exists for your product. Validation of your idea can happen after you have built your minimum viable product (MVP) and tested it out with a few initial customers. Let's discuss how you can go about building your MVP.

BUILDING YOUR MINIMUM VIABLE PRODUCT (MVP)
Assuming you have gone over the chapters on getting into the right mindset, coming up with your idea, and creating your business plan, the next step in the process would be to begin building your minimum viable product. Wikipedia

defines a minimum viable product as "a version of a product with just enough features to be usable by early customers who can then provide feedback for future product development."

A minimum viable product is the bare minimum versIon of the product that will allow you to validate the "viability" of your product. This means you will need to build out the experience of your product to validate how your customers receive it, but the development of the software-based functionality of the product may not have to be built yet.

Building the back-end/logical layer in software development often takes longer than building the front-end/presentation layer. Back-end systems need extensive testing to ensure the product will behave as expected and without glitches. A lot of the effort that goes into building the back-end software can be fulfilled by nonautomated, human efforts for the initial product validation. Building your product this way allows you to do the "minimum" amount of work to validate that your envisioned product can actually be sold to customers.

Depending on the type of product you intend to build, you may be able to test out the product's viability without actually building anything. A popular example of a very successful company that did so was Dropbox. The core functionality of Dropbox heavily relied on the back-end, remote file-sharing software to function correctly, which was complex to build and would have taken months to develop. It was nearly impossible for its founder, Drew Houston, to confirm his hypothesis that Dropbox would be well-received by prospective customers without actually building the entire product.

Since Houston did not want to put in hundreds of hours into building a product no one would want, he came up with a brilliant alternative—he made a video about it. The simple, quirky video explained to customers what Dropbox does and why this new software technology is something most users with multiple devices connected to the internet really needed. Along with the video, Houston also created a website for interested users to enter their email addresses to be added to their beta user waiting list.

The video was an instant hit! Within a few hours, people were flocking to the website to leave their email addresses, giving Drew the validation he was looking for. In a 2011 TechCrunch article by Eric Ries, "How Dropbox Started as a Minimal Viable Product," the founder recounted, "It drove hundreds of thousands of people to the website. Our beta waiting list went from 5,000 people to 75,000 people literally overnight. It totally blew us away."

Another way to gauge customer traction without building any piece of software would be by introducing the concept of your product through existing social media platforms or blogging websites.

Joon Beh, the cofounder of the popular language-learning platform Hallo, started out by testing his idea on Facebook.

> *The reason we were confident in our business model was that we were always talking to users and customers to understand their behaviors and patterns. One thing we realized was there were over fifty million English learners on Facebook, trying to find opportunities to*

speak with other partners. So, they would put a message on Facebook and say, "Hey, I want to practice English with somebody. Who's available?" and they would go to WhatsApp Messenger or Skype to get together and practice.

So we knew there were a lot of people who were trying to find practice partners through Facebook. We were able to validate that through Facebook, and then we built Hallo based on the knowledge we had. In the meantime, we were also testing livestreams on Facebook for language learning. As soon as we released it, our group started growing exponentially. Currently, we have over a million followers, and we haven't spent any money on advertising. So, I think what we did really well at was understanding the problem to solve and testing it without having to build.

In the first one and a half years, we didn't have an actual product, but we were testing many different ideas specifically through Facebook. We were leveraging different platforms to test the ideas. Once we felt like, "Okay, this idea is workinI. there are a ton of people using this. Let's try building it and see how it goes," that's when we were able to start building. As soon as we released it, it started growing and we were able to continue to invest in the product to innovate and continue to make it better.

Joon was able to leverage Facebook to analyze and get data about his potential customers and use the platform to drive connections between the language learners and the language speakers through Hallo's Facebook group. This strategy enabled him to witness the immediate interest of many consumers, which gave him the validation he was seeking before investing more resources into building an actual software product.

Not all MVPs can be made without building at least a basic version of the product. Most times, founders will need to develop a "bare-bones" version of their idea to help them validate it. An example of a business that built a basic software product to test the viability of its idea is Ketto, a cause-oriented crowdfunding platform based out of India which primarily supports social or charitable causes. Ketto's cofounder, Varun Sheth, was working with a limited budget to test his hypothesis that many people would be interested in contributing toward causes from the convenience of their homes by using an online platform.

> *Initially, the budget I was willing to invest was pretty small. So, through a referral, I found this web development agency. For some reason, I don't know how, it just fell into my budget. They were willing to build a prototype, like a 1.0. Of course, we were able to give certain specs and ideas to them.*

> *They also helped us brainstorm over it, in terms of, "What are the key features? What do we want to build?" or, "This is too much, do we want to build so much?" After about twelve months of brainstorming and building, we got a very clunky version out there, which did the basic job of getting somebody to transact to a simple profile.*

Then we got out there. Once it was live, the idea was to go to real customers. When you don't have a product and you go and talk to customers, they will say, "Yeah, this sounds good. We would love to sign up," or, "We would be interested once you are ready, you can get back to us then."

The situation is very different when your product is out there. Just getting them to start acting on it is a different ball game altogether. So, the next year was pretty hard in terms of going to these guys who we had spoken to—trying to convince them, sitting in their office, making sure we did those bi-weekly catch-ups face-to-face at their office, training them, and taking them through the process. We wanted to make sure there is some engagement and traffic on the platform through which we could get some feedback, so it helps us build our 2.0 more efficiently and much better.

Varun knew simply speaking with prospective customers and asking them what they thought of his idea was not good enough. He had to get the first, clunky version out there to understand if the customers who claimed to love the idea would actually use the product. Once he had the 1.0 version of the product ready, he decided to validate it with the biggest customer segment available, the nonprofits. In India, nonprofits are always looking for more support and ways to reach the masses. Varun and his team realized if they could get the nonprofits to collaborate with them, they may find the traction they had been seeking.

Given the large scope of the project, we just broke it down and said, "Which is the one space we can get into which has a low barrier to entry, is not too expensive, where customers are willing to switch to our product quickly and believe in people who are inexperienced and have no idea about their industry?"

We realized, "We want to target nonprofits because there's a massive long tail in a country like India." It would be easy, too, at that point, to create an early dent and to get some kind of a product/market fit. So, we just started making a list of the nonprofits in Mumbai, ones we could connect with through, if not our first network, our second network. We wanted to get some introductions with the right people who would give us the face time with them, so we could get feedback on the product.

We can see from Varun's perseverance to get customers to use Ketto as a platform a big part of building your MVP is not just to build the product and get it out there, but also following up and repeatedly engaging with the initial interested customers, pursuing them to use the product and provide feedback.

Eric Ries, the author of *The Lean Startup*, one of the most popular books about startups, explains the process of iteratively building a product by using what he calls a build-measure-learn feedback loop. Using this technique, entrepreneurs should aim to *build* upon their ideas, *measure* how the product is received by testing it with prospective customers, and use the data from these tests to *learn* how to continue building upon the product. The build-measure-learn feedback loop allows founders to validate their product frequently and regularly with every new version. This allows them to not waste time and resources on building something the market may not want. This type of iterative building is now widely accepted as a standard for building new products.

Building the MVP of your product is similar to going over the build-measure-learn feedback loop for the very first time. As you learn from your MVP, you will use your learnings to gradually create a product that leads you to produce a version that generates maximum customer traction, referred to as product/market fit.

I'll explain product/market fit in the next chapter. For now, let's learn the two steps that go into building your minimum viable product. You will need to:

1. Determine the minimal product to be built.
2. Determine how you will gauge customer traction.

DETERMINE THE MINIMAL PRODUCT TO BE BUILT

To validate how a potential customer would receive your product, you would need to build the user experience for your product's core functionality. The core functionality of your product can be determined by putting your features through the sieve of frugality by really asking yourself if a particular feature will or will not change your target customer's perception of the product.

Start by listing down the features that will impact the core experience of the product. If your product offers multiple core features such as making a reservation, modifying requests, and displaying reviews, start by listing only the most important features you believe will impact how your product is received.

For example, in a reservation system like Airbnb, the set of features would look something like this:

1. My customer should be able to log into the website.
2. My customer should be able to view a list of available listings.
3. My customer should be able to click on a listing to view details about it.
4. My customer should be able to view reviews and ratings of a listing.
5. My customer should be able to make a reservation on a listing for a selected date and time.
6. My customer should be able to pay for the reservation made by entering her payment details.
7. My customer should be able to receive an email regarding the reservation, once confirmed.
8. My customer should be able to leave reviews and ratings on a listing she has previously reserved.
9. My customer should be able to log out of the website.

Now, for each feature, ask yourself the following questions:

1. Is this feature essential for the customer experience?
2. Can this feature be completed manually or by using an existing platform?

IS THIS FEATURE ESSENTIAL FOR THE CUSTOMER EXPERIENCE?

You should be able to answer this question with a binary response—yes or no. If your customer understands and appreciates your startup's concept without the feature, you do not need to build it.

In my reservation system example, I would need to build out the reservation feature first before adding reviews and ratings to the listings. These are essentially two distinct features, one that allows customers to browse through the listings and lets them reserve a selected listing, and one that allows customers to add reviews and ratings to a listing. Even if I believe both the features are core to my customer's experience, can I delay building out the reviews and ratings feature until after I have tested that I have a market for the reservation feature?

Look over your own set of features in a similar way. Which features need to be built first before the other features can be built? Can you begin testing after the first feature is built? Chop off all the features that can be built in a later iteration.

If I did this exercise for my reservation system example, I would filter down my list of features to:

1. My customer should be able to view a list of available listings.
2. My customer should be able to click on a listing to view details about it.
3. My customer should be able to make a reservation on a listing for a selected date and time.
4. My customer should be able to pay for the reservation made by entering her payment details.
5. My customer should be able to receive an email regarding the reservation once confirmed.

Now, moving on to the next question.

Can This Feature Be Completed Manually or by Using an Existing Platform?

In this step, you will need to further filter down your features by determining whether your startup's concept can be validated by using an existing platform or by manually completing the work offered by the feature.

Reneta Jenik, the founder of Foodom, an online marketplace for connecting local, vetted chefs with people who want meals prepared in their kitchen, explained how she built the very first version of Foodom using Weebly.

> I was thinking, "How do I make it lean without paying a developer?" because it was just in alpha. I wanted to see if the concept was even working. It's one thing, me not getting a salary, but now, paying a developer? I thought, let's reduce that cost as well.
>
> Then, one day, my gardener came home, and I told him about my business. I showed him the laundry room, where my office is, and he's like, "You know, I'm also now in the process of leaving a big company. I opened my own gardening business." Then he told me, "I'm building a website using Wix," and I'm like, "Really? Who is building this website for you?" He said, "Myself," and I was like, "Really?"
>
> He said it was very low cost. So, I thought, "If he can do it, I can do it too." I mean, we're both nontechnical.

He was in sIs... so it seemed like we have similar backgrounds. So, I needed to check it out, and I did. I checked Wix versus Weebly, but Weebly was much simpler.

Anyway, for simplicity in Weebly, I built a website. It was far away from doing what IInted... I was on the $18 plan from them. I couldn't do the billing through them, so I did all the invoices with PayPal for free. Obviously, there was a processing fee which the customers paid for with a service fee. Then, I found a software in Florida—they did like a personal chef type of software.

So basically, I would get an order on Weebly, I would take it manually, create the operations on this platform [from Florida] that was $35Ir month... I said, "It's just a few orders. Let me test it. I'll do the work manually. If it doesn't work out, it isn't worth spending money on developing [the product]." So, in the software, I would create the work order and the shopping list, and then I'll send the customer an invoice through PayPal, and the customer paid before the chef showed up. It was all manual. After one hundred orders, I decided to develop a product.

All that was like two hours of work for a single order. First creating the orderIhen PayPal... and the day I got two or three orders, I was like, "Shoot me now! Then when I finally decided to invest in the platform, I told the developers, First of all, automatic orders, automatic payments, automatic shopping list. I don't want to do this again!"

Reneta found an effective combination of manual work and preexisting automated software to help her confirm there is a market for the product she was envisioning. She had to come up with some creative ways to make it all work, but she managed to put something together to test out her hypothesis.

In my reservation system example, can I also use an existing payments platform like PayPal for customers to make payments? Of course, if my customers love my product, I can look into integrating my website with a better solution, like a software-based payments framework. I do not *need* to build it for my MVP. Look over your own filtered-down features to determine whether third-party software can handle the functionality for you in an efficient manner.

Now, say I still believe reviews and ratings are essential for the customer experience. If I believe customers would flock to my website because of the transparency of reviews and ratings on each listing, maybe I could manually collect reviews and ratings from customers via email and stage them on my website, as though they were created through software? Look through your own features; can you find any that can be staged for your MVP?

Think of more features that can simply be replaced by manual action. For example, suppose I want my reservation system to send a confirmation email after a customer successfully reserves a booking. For every confirmed reservation, maybe I can manually send out a confirmation email to them?

When I'm done with this exercise, the list of features that would form my MVP will be filtered down to:

1. My customer should be able to view a list of available listings.
2. My customer should be able to click on a listing to view details about it.
3. My customer should be able to make a reservation on a listing for a selected date and time.
4. My customer should use an existing payment service like PayPal to pay for the reservation.

To provide a "complete" customer experience, these are the things I would need to do manually:

1. Send out a confirmation email with a confirmation reference number and an invoice.
2. Request for payments using an existing payments service.
3. Collect reviews for existing listings from customers and add them manually to the website.

DETERMINE HOW YOU WILL GAUGE CUSTOMER TRACTION

As you are building your MVP, you can begin engaging with potential customers. In this step, you would need to slowly start building a network of initial interested customers who would be happy to test out your product for you. Begin by tapping into your network of friends, colleagues, and family. If there are specific online groups where many of your target customers are active, post on these groups to find out if anyone would be interested in testing your product.

There is no incorrect time to communicate with potential customers. Ideally, you should begin engaging with them even before your MVP is built, so you garner some initial interest in your product. Begin this process as early as you can, so you have already sort of tested the waters as you build your MVP.

You should begin by creating a list of beta customers who are the right fit for your target market. These are the people who will help you find that sweet spot in your product to help you gain traction. Engage with these beta customers regularly as your MVP is getting built—giving them an idea of what to expect, what to test, and what sort of feedback you are looking for.

When Reneta was building Foodom, she took every opportunity to get feedback from her customers. She was excited to hear what she could do to improve upon the product, and eventually went on to ask every customer for reviews on their experience with the chefs, the food, and the service:

> *I'm speaking with every customer that is willing to talk to me. I'm reaching out to any new customer who makes a booking on Foodom. With the people I know, it's easier. With the people I don't know, almost all of them talk to me and give me feedback. Not a lot of them feel comfortable telling me bad things, but I'm like, "It's good, it's good, please tell me." They're very sweet customers. We now also ask customers for reviews on a regular basis, their reviews on Foodom, on the chef, and on the dishes.*

Asking for feedback is a skill in itself. A simple "How did you like it?" does not suffice. Reneta recommends a book called

The Mom Test by Rob Fitzpatrick, which she uses to under-stand her customers' behaviors better. The concept behind *The Mom Test* is you should ask customers the type of ques-tions even your mom, who loves everything you do, will have to answer with complete honesty. It allows businesses to learn more about customer behavior and their environments and enables them to take note of potential points of failure in their business.

Here are some questions that apply *The Mom Test* concept I can use for my product:
- What do you usually use the product for?
- When was the last time you used the product? To do what?
- How did you solve this problem before the prod-uct existed?
- How did you find out about us?
- Do you use any other products to solve the same problem?

You can also learn how your beta customers are using your product by simply being present when they use your product. Request some (or all) of your beta customers if you can watch them as they navigate through the different features of your product. Note down where they seem to be spending the most time, where they seem to be confused about what to do next, and where they seem to act quickly as if they already knew where a particular button was. Observe their reaction as they use your product. Do they seem satisfied with what the product provides them? Or are they simply doing this as a chore because you asked them to? If you have chosen your beta customers appropriately, you should be able to tell if they get excited after using even a clunky, incomplete ver-sion of your product. If the product you are building is truly engaging or valuable, your beta customers should have a lot to say about it.

Using this feedback from beta customers, continue iterating over your product. Make the experience better if they seemed to find parts of it unintuitive, add features that were requested by a majority of them. With each new improvement or an added feature, continue to gauge customer reaction and learn from it.

As you learn, you may realize a majority of them do not find your product exciting or useful enough to pay for it or even use it often. It is possible your initial idea is not taking off as you had expected. Your assumptions about what your target market wants may have been proven incorrect as you go through the steps highlighted in this chapter.

Since you were iteratively building upon your product and validating your assumptions as you went along, these learnings should come early enough in the process that you don't feel like you have wasted too much time and effort. Through these learnings, you may also feel like you know the product better and know what to do differently the next time around. Sometimes, with just a few tweaks to your initial product, you may be able to create a product that really appeals to the market. This is called a pivot, and we'll discuss it in the next chapter.

CHAPTER SUMMARY

- A minimum viable product (MVP) is the bare minimum version of the product that will allow you to learn if your product will be received well by customers.

- You do not need to build software to determine the viability of your product. You may be able to test it out by using existing tools or social media platforms.

- The process of building your MVP comprises of two steps:
  - Determine the minimal product to be built.
  - Determine how you will gauge customer traction.

- Building the minimal presentation layer involves asking two important questions about each feature you intend to build:
  - Is this feature essential for the customer experience?
  - Can this feature be completed manually or by using an existing platform?

- To gauge customer traction:
  - Connect with your network to collect a set of initial beta customers who will be willing to test a minimal version of the product for you.
  - Perform in person observations of how some of your beta customers use your product and navigate through its features.

- Collect feedback from customers by asking specific questions they will need to answer honestly like:
  - What do you usually use the product for?
  - When was the last time you used the product? To do what?

- How did you solve this problem before the product existed?
- How did you find out about us?
- Do you use any other products to solve the same problem?

THE STARTUP EVOLUTION—THE ROAD TO PRODUCT/ MARKET FIT

"The product that wins is the one that bridges customers to the future, not the one that requires a giant leap."

—AARON LEVIE

Varun couldn't believe his eyes. He had been closely monitoring the numbers on his screen for the last few hours, and now it seemed like they were rising exponentially. His company, Ketto, a crowdfunding platform for cause-oriented campaigns, had an open campaign for one of India's star athletes, Shiva Keshavan. Shiva's goal for the campaign was to raise one million Indian Rupees to buy top-class equipment for the fifth Winter Olympics to compete with other athletes at a global level with the best equipment. With the help of Ketto, Shiva was able to set up his campaign and requested his fellow Indians to contribute toward what could lead to a national win for the country.

Varun was looking at the numbers rolling in. This was turning out to be one of Ketto's most successful campaigns. The metrics showed more people than ever before were logging on to their platform to donate. It wasn't just that. People were leaving comments about how much they liked the website and were surprised they hadn't heard of it before. Many of the website's visitors even visited other campaign events to see which other causes Ketto supported, and at times, even contributed to them.

Varun was now seeing the Olympian's campaign was going viral. There were social media posts everywhere with Ketto's donation link with people encouraging their friends and family to donate. Some of Varun's friends were also messaging him personally to congratulate him on such a well-designed website.

"This is going to change how India contributes to social causes," they said. Shiva Keshavan, the Olympian, managed to accomplish his goal of raising one million Indian Rupees. He was thrilled! Ketto had brought this young luge player closer to his dreams.

I think it was only after three years when we got this one big breakthrough. This massive campaign, it was the biggest one at the time, which took three years to happen. This athlete's campaign happened on the platform, and we got a decent amount of money, but we also got a lot of PR around it. It made a lot of noise. Customers who used the platform loved it and shared pretty good feedback. It just went viral.

A lot of people who came and transacted gave us feedback like, "Wow, we didn't know this existed. This was so easy to do. Why didn't anybody tell us about this before? How can we do more?" So that was the first inflection point we were looking for when we got a decent amount of people transacting in a short period of time. That gave us the confidence and helped us close on a small outside funding round when we knew what kind of a 2.0 we wanted to build.

From that learning, we just got down to building a 2.0 version. By the time we had a 2.0 out, we had found a decent amount of product/market fit. I would say that was when the traction really started picking up, and things started to get exciting.

It took about a year for Varun and his team to build the 1.0 version of the product, which they used for initial testing. Between the twelve months and three years when he realized they had finally created a product the market loved, Varun was working on honing and fine-tuning his product, learning from his customers, retooling, and reviewing newer versions.

It was a mix of a few things. We were interacting with organizations like the nonprofits and taking a lot of feedback from them which helped us build a better 2.0.

Of course, it always seems like these things will happen overnight, but it takes time.

We were able to convert some big organizations over the period of those two to three years by constantly knocking on their door and asking them to use the platform as a service. So, those kinds of things started falling into place after a couple of years.

At that point in time, we had built a 2.0, which seemed like it was ahead of anything that was in the market at that point in time. So, a lot of these large organizations loved the product and gave us some great feedback. That got things rolling.

So it was a mix of all the feedback we had accumulated, knocking on doors for the first couple of years, those things converting, and some money to fasten our product development.

Once the campaign was over, Varun reflected on how everyone had reacted. He was, of course, delighted at everyone's responses and was excited to see Ketto get so much traction. He was also quick to realize it took him and his team three years to get to this day. For the people of India, Ketto was the new, exciting website they could use to browse and donate to social causes. For Varun, this had been a long and arduous journey, one he could now see ending well.

Today, Ketto is one of India's top crowdfunding platforms. Through the COVID-19 pandemic in India, Ketto had numerous campaigns to collect funds for frontline workers, hospital equipment, etc. In fact, Ketto also got a lot of social media attention when top celebrities used the platform to set up their own COVID-19 relief initiatives.

Varun and his team worked hard to iteratively build an online platform that is intuitive, easy to use, and consumer-friendly. Their idea took three years to get in front of a wide audience and thereafter has only seen growth year after year. In 2020, primarily due to the COVID-19 pandemic, the company grew by four times in a matter of seven months. Needless to say, Ketto is a company that found product/market fit.

But what is product/market fit?

WHAT IS PRODUCT/MARKET FIT?

Product/market fit is a milestone in your startup when the market accepts your product with the least amount of resistance.

We can say a company has found product/market fit when it has discovered the secret formula which allows it to enjoy further growth and success without trying much harder. The customers of such companies will voluntarily use their products because they find them valuable and also tell others about them.

Marc Andreessen initially coined the term in his 2007 blog post, "The only thing that matters," where he defined product/market fit as "being in a good market with a product that can satisfy that market."

For every new startup, the goal is to find product/market fit through the iterative process of learning from customer and expert feedback and fine-tuning your product to fit better and better with the market's needs. When you have found product/market fit, your customers will often claim to have found exactly what they needed. Let me put this in a few different examples to demonstrate what product/market fit looks like better:

- If you see a particular version of your product has drastically driven up your product's engagement and adoption metrics, you may have found product/market fit.
- If your customers are ready to use broken or half-completed versions of your product because it saves them time and the alternative approaches are too complicated or clunky to use, you may have found a product/market fit.
- If your customers are ready to pay for your product, and you have no difficulty convincing them this product is indeed valuable, you may have found a product/market fit.

Arjun Sundararajan, the founder of Zync, an interactive platform for running engaging virtual events, describes product/market fit with a common example that's used in the startup circles:

> I would say startups are in two phases. The preproduct/market fit stage and the postproduct/market fit stage. They are both two very different beasts. You probably have heard of this analogy before where the preproduct/market fit feels like you're pushing this big boulder up a mountain and trying to get everybody aligned. The challenge is to not slip and to put a lot of heavy work into it. The postproduct/market fit is when

you've reached the peak, and this ball is now rolling down, and it's so hard to control it. There's a different type of craziness about it where you're trying to keep everything in order.

The analogy is so simple yet makes the concept very easy to understand. In the preproduct/market fit stage, which is similar to pushing this boulder uphill, you're still working on getting enough customers to like your product. You're probably going to get exhausted or burned out while you figure out how to build the product well enough to suit your customer's needs. You may even have a hard time building the right team, getting them aligned and executing effectively, and learning from customer feedback. After you have successfully pushed this proverbial boulder up to the peak, it starts rolling down with full force. This is when you get to the postproduct/market fit stage. In this stage, you know the product satisfies the market's needs, and your customers are willing to purchase the product and spread awareness about it. The pace of your company will pick up, and it'll seem like more and more customers are flocking to use your product. You will now need to think about how to scale—hiring more people, acquiring more funding, and keeping this boulder rolling. There's a different type of struggle here. You will be struggling to control your boulder, which is now rolling down from the hill so fast it's almost rolling away from you.

Let's talk about how your product can get closer to achieving product/market fit.

HOW CAN YOU FIND PRODUCT/MARKET FIT?

From the time you get your very first customer feedback to the time you achieve product/market fit, the process involves three primary steps:

- Fine-tuning
- Pivoting
- Seeking expert advice

In this chapter, I will cover the fine-tuning and pivot aspects. You will learn more about seeking expert advice in "The Startup Network—Investors, Advisors, and Accelerators."

FINE-TUNING

As you learn from initial customer feedback from your MVP, you will go through the process of fine-tuning. That is, you will be making improvements to your product based on recommendations and suggestions from your customers. This can either be as small as changing up the placement of a button on your website to make it more visible or may also be more significant, like introducing a new feature your customers have been requesting.

In the process of fine-tuning, you will still build toward the same vision where you will continue to work toward finding a product/market fit with the same target market. The features you provide or the way you present information to your customers may change slightly based on customer feedback, but you are still inherently trying to solve the same problem for the same set of customers.

Arjun Vora, the cofounder of Zira, the online workforce management platform for hourly workers and their employers, explains how his team went about fine-tuning their product:

I think there was this higher level of understanding we had because of our early interviews with all the Uber drivers, which was like, you want flexibility. That was the essence of it. That right now, that flexibility in their voice is not there. So, that was the hypothesis we wanted to address. Then there were the individual customers who we onboarded early on, even before the product was built as design partners. We spoke to them very deeply about the problems their businesses were having. We also went around malls and the AMC theaters and retail shops and spoke to the employees with a design prototype. We were like, "What if I gave you this? Will this solve your problems?"

I remember going into the Levi's store in Berkeley, and that person removed a binder of a schedule. She was like, "Mary Anne comes on this day." I was like, "Wow, you guys are still using this? Why?" Then she brought up all the pain points. She was like, "You know, Tuesdays she forgets she has to come at 9:15, and on some other day she forgets she has to come in at 9:45."

So, we got thinking. How do we automate not only some of the scheduling, so she's not given that shift but also some of the notifications around it? Going directly to our user base and chatting with them helps. I remember going to another retail store where an employee was like, "You know, I don't know how much I'm going to get paid at the end of my two weeks. That's a big problem for me because my partner and I need to plan our finances, and we can't plan our finances this way."

We take so many of these things for granted ourselves— like we have money in the bank, and we have a fixed salary coming in every time. So, we created this feature where the employees could track in real-time how much they're going to make and what it's forecasted for. It's like, "On Sunday, this is how much you will get paid." Stuff like that we built through those learnings we got when taking these prototypes to these employees.

As you learn from your initial testers, you will iteratively build newer versions of your product, taking you closer and closer to achieving product/market fit. All startups go through this process of learning from feedback, reviewing what's important for the customers, and retooling based on the feedback.

As long as your customers seem to want to continue using the product and give you enough indicators that you are heading in the right direction, you can continue to fine-tune and improve upon your product. Let's look at how you can get indications for fine-tuning from your customers.

Beta Testers

To fine-tune your product well, you will need a set of trusted initial customers who are willing to test out and provide feedback for every version of the product you offer them. These customers will form your group of beta testers. You are likely to find multiple volunteers for beta testers within your close network—like your friends, colleagues, or family. Include these people in your pool of testers if they have relevant experience or can provide meaningful feedback.

You will also need some real customers to become beta testers—people who want your product so badly they will use and provide feedback on initial, clunky versions of your product. With each iteration of fine-tuning, attempt to add more beta testers into your pool to ensure you are not building your product for very specific requirements only a handful of your customers have.

When you present a new version of your product to these beta testers, ask them precise questions like:
- Which feature do you use the most?
- When do you use the product? How often?
- Which feature would you say is missing from this product?
- Which feature, according to you, adds the most value to the product?
- Does this version address some or all your concerns about the previous version of the product?
- Was the user interface on this version easier to use?
- Which parts of the user interface seemed slow or unintuitive?
- How many stars would you give to the product between one and five?

Leave the feedback open-ended, allow your beta testers to give additional suggestions, even if the suggestions may not align with your product's vision. These suggestions will provide you with much insight into how your product can change course if your current vision is not materializing the way you expected it to.

On a spreadsheet, note down feedback from these beta testers in different rows, with each of their responses and additional suggestions. Keep an eye out for the same type of feedback from multiple testers. Are multiple testers requesting a single improvement or a single missing feature? Do multiple testers find a single page on your user interface unintuitive to use?

Once you collect this feedback and note it down, rank the suggestions for improvements or features in descending order, starting from the most to the least requested. Analyze and estimate how much effort each improvement/feature will take in terms of time. If you do not have the technical expertise to make such estimations, use an expert to guide you. If you have hired a specialized team to work on the software for your product, use the technical lead's help to make rough estimations.

In addition to time, you also want to estimate if any of the items on your list require you to hire professionals to complete the work. If applicable, add an additional field for cost estimations.

Once you have completed this exercise, use your findings as your primary guide for making the necessary changes to the next iteration of your product. Determine how you may want to address the top three to five items on your list. Your aim should be to deliver the next version within a fixed amount of time, say, two months. Work backward from a date to determine how many of your top fine-tuning tasks can be completed before the date. Give your beta testers a heads up about what's coming up and when to be prepared to test the next version. You want to do this to keep up the engagement, so they feel heard and like you're bringing them along in the process.

Analyze Your Competition
Fine-tuning of your product can also be done by simply analyzing the competition. You would have done this in your ideation phase, but in your fine-tuning phase, you can do it at a level deeper to determine what makes your competition click.

Saumya Shah, the founder of Tarrakki, an online wealth management platform based out of India, decided to look at similar apps within the country and the US.

> *I used to sign up for products that were in India. I would compare them with how they were built in the US. It could be something as simple as how the user interface or the onboarding experience was. So, I was constantly comparing different platforms. It could be something very simple, like how they place a call-to-action button on the app. The position of the button is important because if your customer is looking at the page, you want them to click on it. I will say it is very important to do some level of such research.*

Looking through similar products will give you an insight into what works from a user experience perspective for your target customers. It would make sense to sign up for and use some of your competing products to understand which user interface elements and specific features you can adopt from them. Be sure to check if any of the features have been patented by other companies and need specific licensing. Additionally, looking through customer reviews of similar products will also help you understand why customers use the product. This, in turn, will give you additional insight into the parts of your app that may not be working very well for your customers.

PIVOT

As you continue to build upon your product, you may realize your product is not receiving the traction you expected. You may either feel like your product's progress has hit a plateau, and you cannot see your startup grow much further, or your product seems like it does not hold much value to your customers.

Eric Ries, an American entrepreneur and author of *The Lean Startup*, and Steve Blank, also an American entrepreneur, educator, speaker, and author, coined the term "pivot" as a part of the Lean Startup Movement. He defined it as a "structured course correction designed to test a new fundamental hypothesis about the product, strategy, and engine of growth."

If you have spent enough time fine-tuning your product and appealing to your target customers but you're still not seeing traction, it is likely you will need to make bigger changes to the product to make it fit better with the market's needs. Your learnings from the evolution phases thus far may have led you to some specific conclusions about the product, like the possibility of getting more traction if you narrowed your target customer profile some more, or if you built further upon one main feature all your customers seem to love, or if you solved an entirely different problem you discovered a lot of your customers have by analyzing their feedback. In such cases, you should consider a pivot.

Helena Ronis is the founder of AllFactors, a web analytics software for businesses to drive marketing and growth. Before she founded AllFactors, Helena worked at a startup that started out as a consumer app for celebrities to communicate in real-time with their fans using a livestreaming technology that was built in-house. The startup's goal was to become popular by getting a lot of users to visit the app, which they could then use to drive up the engagement. This concept is similar to how other social media apps of today thrive in the market.

They made a mistake in their business model. They assumed users would keep coming back to rewatch live sessions from the past. From their observations, it was clear users were only visiting the platform when their favorite celebrities were live on it but did not seem interested in rewatching live interactions from the past. By looking over their metrics, they saw they could not create the same kind of engagement as the popular social media apps. Moreover, they were spending large amounts of money to get these celebrities to participate in the live interactions, which, in turn, was driving the business to the ground.

Eventually, when they went back to the drawing board to think through their business model, they realized they needed a change in direction to continue growing as a company. Looking through the different parts of the business, they saw their livestreaming technology was superior and very well-built.

They decided to use it as an opportunity to pivot and started providing the technology to organizations like colleges and small businesses that needed to host live events.

To understand pivots more clearly, let's look at the different cases in which you should and should not consider a pivot.

When to Pivot?

The decision to pivot can lead to major changes in the product you have built so far, so you should only consider pivoting if you are sure the product you are building will not be able to scale any further. Look for indications from your customers and your metrics. I'll talk more about metrics in the chapter "The Startup Measurements."

Let's take Naama Moran, for example. Na'ama is the cofounder of multiple tech startups like Cheetah and Sourcery, and Cheetah evolved as a pivot from her learnings from Sourcery. Na'ama started Sourcery from a personal interest to work with business owners in the food space. Her father was a farmer and later owned his own bakery, so she felt a deep personal connection toward problems in the food space. She created Sourcery, which was intended to be an online purchasing platform that connected wholesale foodservice buyers like corporate kitchens and restaurant groups with their wholesale foodservice suppliers like big foodservice distributors or smaller local distributors. As she continued building the product, she found some interesting insights that led her to pivot.

> *What I found out about a year and a half later is despite the fact we had a ton of demand on the buyers' side, where buyers really wanted these types of tools*

and transparency and content reach information and user-friendly experience, I just could not get the vendorIo participate... In many cases, these were large food service distributors that just did not want to share their prices because they were benefiting from the fact that there was no price transparency. On the other side—the small ones, like farmers or small distributors—they wanted to get access to these buyers and wanted to participate in my platform but didn't have enough sophistication to actually be in an e-commerce platform. I would need their inventory information, but they would have no way to provide that. So, we needed to ultimately create a ton of scrapers to manage scraping and extracting data from spreadsheets and PDF to create the catalog for them.

So, I realized that was not very scalable. The long story short is there was a quarter at the beginning of 2014 when I was plunging my whole team into finding a pivot for Sourcery's ordering platform into something thatIuld scale better... I came to the conclusion that with the vendors not wanting to participate in the marketplace, even though I have this traction on the buyers' side, I'm just not going to get the marketplace dynamic I was expecting to get.

Ultimately, I came out with two different ideas. One of them was turning the ordering platform into an invoice management platform because I said, "Well, if the vendors don't want to be part of working with us, let's do something where we don't need the vendors' help but still provide value to restaurants." So, with *invoice management, the buyers, which are the restaurants, would simply be able to upload their invoices, we would scan the invoices, extract pricing information, and then we would show them how prices of commodities fluctuate. It was more in hindsight, but it still gave them a very good negotiating tool to go back to the vendors and say, "Hey, why is my price on milk higher? You told me it's going to be $5 per gallon and now it's $6 just a week later." You know? We gave them the tool to keep their vendors honest. Then, we also enabled them to pay their vendors online. So, they moved to online payments, and we integrated that with their accounting systems, where we literally took the whole hassle of managing paper invoices and digitized it for them.*

The other idea I was doing was I figured if I can't change the behavior of the vendor, how could I create a better vendor experience? Can I find a vendor that is, by definition, price transparent? I found there was a very large vendor for restaurants called Restaurants Depot. It's like Sam's Club or Costco, but it's focused on restaurants. It's a very large company. They have about 150 warehouses all over the country, and they have a price transparent model because it's a retail store. So, everyone who goes there gets the same prices from the shelf. They don't have delivery, though. It's a retail store, right? Restaurants have to go there, do all the shopping on their own, and deliver.

So I figured, why don't we do something like Instacart for restaurants? I already had an online ordering system, so I had that technology. So, we were able to bootstrap their catalog by literally scraping their website. We also had customers with who we were able to test this concept, and customers really loved it. So, then I was able to network my way and get in touch with the executive team at Restaurant Depot. I basically said, "Why don't we do that? I have an ordering system, I have customers, I've tested it, and they like it. Can you give me access to your catalog? I'll be just going into your store, picking up, and doing deliveries." They were like, "Sure, let's do it." I was very lucky.

So, they gave me access to their API, which is also kind of amazing in itself that they actually had an API. We were able to integrate their API into our ordering platform. Later on, we developed a mobile application. That was the beginning of Cheetah, my current company.

Na'ama's primary learning from Sourcery was that restaurant food vendors did not like to be price transparent because it hurt their business. She was able to take this insight and find a wholesale retail vendor who was price transparent by definition and integrate a delivery model into it. Essentially, Na'ama was working with two sets of target customers: the vendors and the buyers. With the pivot, she continued to address the same problem and the same set of buyers but changed her vendors to ultimately find product/market fit through Cheetah.

If you answer yes to one or more of the following questions, there may be indications that a pivot will help your product find product/market fit.

Are you losing more money than you are making? Do you see that not changing?

This may be the case if your product uses the hidden revenue business model when you are waiting for your customer base to scale rapidly so you can make money from targeted advertising. If your product does not take off as expected even after you've tried hard to make it appealing to your customers, you may never be able to scale it enough to attract advertisers. In these types of situations, it may be wise to consider a pivot.

Are you constantly being outperformed by your competition?

If you are in a market where there are many other similar products that essentially provide the same features and core functionality as your product, you may find yourself constantly being outperformed by your competition. If your competition existed in the market before your product was launched, customers who use your competition as their "default" option may not see an incentive to switch over to using your product. In such cases, you may want to decide if pivoting may be the right decision by looking into your growth metrics and determining whether you have hit a plateau and do not see much further growth ahead.

Do customers only seem to like a single feature of your product?

If you receive beta testing feedback that indicates many of them really like a single feature of the product but do not seem to care enough about the other features to give much feedback, you may want to spend more time centering your product around this feature.

Instagram is a famous example of a company that was formed this way. According to a June 2020 article by Dan Blystone on Investopedia, "The Story of Instagram: The Rise of the #1 Photo-Sharing Application," when Instagram was started, its name was originally Burbn. Founder Kevin Systrom built Burbn as a location-based check-in web app where people could go to post their travel plans and check-in when they're at different locations. One of the features the app provided was photo sharing. Upon assessing customer feedback and reviews, Systrom and his team realized the photo-sharing feature was extremely popular among Burbn users. They eventually decided to center their app around just that feature and add more to it like likes and comments and renamed it Instagram in 2010. Within a couple of months, their number of users grew to a million. When Facebook bought Instagram in 2012 for $1 billion, the app had scaled up to a user base of approximately twenty-seven million.

Is there a limited response from your customers?
If you have tried incorporating feedback from various customers and building the product to the best of your ability over multiple months and are still not seeing enough of a response from your customers, it may be a good time to consider a pivot. This probably just means the market does not find your product interesting or valuable enough to use frequently. This could also be related to your product's timing. Maybe your product is too ahead of its time, and the market is not ready for it yet.

Slack's founder Stewart Butterfield started a business to launch a game called "Glitch," which was intended to be the primary product offered to customers. Glitch only managed to get a few ardent followers, but it did not become a popular game despite many efforts. To cut losses, Butterfield and his team decided to pivot on the product entirely. While building the game, the developers on the team were spread across different cities like San Francisco, New York, and Vancouver. To communicate with each other effectively, they created an internal chat system that worked so well for them it became one of the most popular tools. Seeing great potential in what his team had built internally, Butterfield decided to launch the tool as Slack. It was built to serve as an internal chat tool within corporations. Sure enough, the idea clicked. According to a blog post on Nira by Hiten Shah, "How Slack Became a $16 Billion Business by Making Work Less Boring," within a matter of two years, their daily active users grew from 14,600 in 2014 after launch to three million in 2016.

Has your vision or passion for the product changed?
As you build your product, your passion and vision for the original product will likely change as you learn more. You may learn about different applications of your product or different ways of how your product can be used from your beta testers and research. This may make you want to build toward a different vision. It is also possible your passion for building the original product is not the same. You could find out, after spending enough time building the product, the original idea does not resonate with you anymore. In this case, pivoting could be a difficult decision because it may still make sense to create the product you envisioned for your customers if you have many customers interested in using it.

While there is no right answer here, the feedback and metrics you have collected should help you decide if pivoting makes sense for you.

That being said, there are reasons *not* to pivot as well. Let's look into those.

When to NOT Pivot
If you haven't spent enough time fine-tuning your product to verify it *cannot* take off, you should not pivot.

Suppose you're feeling demotivated or discouraged by the lack of customer responses but haven't put in enough effort into collecting feedback, analyzing it, and creating improved versions of your product. If that is the case, you may be pivoting too early.

It's easy to get discouraged when you do not see quick gratification for your efforts. We live in a world where we're continually being subjected to instant gratification fueled by the many social media platforms. You may find yourself in a situation where you want to give up on your original plan and chase a different idea you think is trending or taking off right now. It is also possible you feel like you should have seen some positive results with all the efforts you have already taken. Avoid the temptation to pivot too soon until you have ensured you have taken all the efforts you possibly could to make your product work.

How to Pivot?
You can think of pivoting as keeping the parts of your product that work well and changing the ones that do not. Pay

close attention to the parts of your business that have garnered positive reactions from your initial customers. If you use those parts and expand from there, you will likely find the right combination of features to make your product click. Let's talk about some ways to pivot.

By focusing on the single, most popular feature of the product

Work Human is a company that broke into the exclusive league of unicorns (companies with billion-dollar valuations) in mid-2020. The company was created first as an online gift-giving service before it pivoted to become a cloud-based service designed for employees in global workplaces to reward and recognize each other.

In a November 2020 podcast interview with Brené Brown, "Brené with Eric Mosley on Making Work Human," the company's founder, Eric Mosley, shared how the idea evolved by zooming into a single unique aspect of their initial product. "We had the idea for a global gift-giving service for consumers and businesses, but what happened was businesses latched on to it and started to use that service for incentives and recognition programs for their employees. So, we realized this is where you could build a scalable business, and that's where it all started. We pivoted into just the corporate world from that gift-giving service and started to innovate around recognition and what it could be in culture management, in creating community and culture in companies," shared Mosley.

By looking at customer feedback, if you begin to notice a single feature is getting a lot of attention and love, you may want to focus all your developer efforts into making that piece the core of your platform's functionality. Create a set of features that can enhance this popular feature to make it more appealing. Make the feature and its sub-features the main highlight of your product. Continue to monitor how customers react to the changes to determine whether you're gaining traction.

The journey from Burbn to Instagram also fits perfectly here. Kevin Systrom and his team decided to "zoom in" on their initial location-based check-in app's single, most popular feature.

By changing the problem

If you never saw much customer traction for your product, it is likely you are not solving a real problem people actually have. This may happen in most cases where your startup product or idea is entertainment or engagement-oriented and not really a pressing problem that needs to be solved. It's likely customers are not finding it entertaining enough, or competitors in the space have already captured the target market.

Look within the product you have built and determine if you can use some of the things you have built to solve a different problem. The Slack example fits perfectly here. Slack's business team saw the game they were creating was not getting interest from many customers. So, they decided to pivot to creating their internal chat tool, the centerpiece of their product. From what they learned from the metrics, they realized the internal chat tool would receive more traction than the game and hence decided to work on a different problem by using technology they had already built well.

By changing your target customers

Suppose you have built a product for a specific target market but do not see enough traction from the market. If your product can be applied to a related but different market and continue to solve the same problem, you should consider this option.

Na'ama Moran's pivot that led her to create Cheetah was achieved by switching from traditional restaurant food vendors to retail stores that were wholesale food providers for restaurants. This pivot gave her buyers the price transparency and consistent pricing model they could not find from the traditional vendors.

Another way to know if you should focus on a different customer segment is by observing the type of people your product attracts. For example, according to an Aug 2014 article on The Verge, "Justin.tv, the live video pioneer that birthed Twitch, officially shuts down," Michael Seibel, the cofounder of Twitch, started his startup with his cofounders as Justin TV, which was a website that showed a livestreaming video of one of their friends and fellow cofounder, Justin. Eventually, Justin TV allowed other customers to also livestream their daily lives on video, which brought them some interest from customers. Even as they saw traction from customers, the founders did not see how the product could be scaled further.

They also observed that a significant chunk of the interested users really liked watching livestreams of gamers playing different games. Using this insight as an indication, they decided to pivot by focusing on the livestreams of only the gamers in action. As soon as the product was launched as Twitch, they immediately saw their customer growth metrics go up.

This example shows multiple types of pivots to create a single, successful product, where the founders focused on a single feature and addressed a specific, "zoomed in" target market. According to a 2014 article on Business Insider, "Twitch CEO: Here's Why We Sold to Amazon For $970 Million," within three years of launching Twitch, it had fifty-five million users, and the product was eventually sold to Amazon for a whopping $970 million.

Fine-tuning and pivoting are essential elements in the evolution of a startup until the company finds product/market fit. Another significant element a company can hone over time is figuring out its unique, secret sauces to create an ultimate recipe for success. Let's look into this in the next chapter!

CHAPTER SUMMARY:
- For every new startup, the goal is to find product/market fit through the iterative process of learning from customer feedback and fine-tuning the product to fit the market's needs better.
- The process of finding product/market fit involves three primary steps:
  - Fine-tuning—Learning from customer feedback and honing your product.
  - Pivot—Changing directions by either changing the problem or your target customers or by zooming in on a single feature of your product.
  - Seeking expert advice—Learn from the experiences of experts in the same domain. This will be discussed further in a later chapter.

- Fine-tuning is the process of making improvements to your product based on the recommendations and suggestions from your customers. In the process of fine-tuning, you will still build toward the same vision where you will continue to work with the same target market.
- Fine-tuning is done by having open conversations with beta customers, analyzing what your competition does well, and incorporating the findings to create a better product for your customers.
- If you have spent enough time fine-tuning your product and appealing to your target customers but still not seeing traction, you will likely need to make bigger changes to the product to fit the market's needs better. This is called a pivot.
- A pivot should be considered when:
  - You are losing more money than you are making, and you do not see that changing.
  - Your competition is constantly outperforming you.
  - Customers only seem to like a single feature of your product.
  - There is limited traction for your product from your customers.
  - Your perspective toward your product has changed, and the idea no longer resonates with you.

- A pivot should not be considered if you have not spent enough time and have taken enough effort to get customer traction.
- You can pivot by:
  - Focusing on the single, most popular feature of the product
  - By changing the problem you are solving with your product
  - By changing your target customers

THE STARTUP JAZZ

———

Imagine listening to your favorite song as you relax on a plush chair by a beautiful window with sun pouring in as the many trees outside sway gently with the breeze. Imagine sitting there and observing the beauty surrounding you as you soak in the music like it is almost speaking to you.

Now imagine creating the same experience for your customers, where your customers are absolutely delighted to be using your product and can't stop talking about it to their friends and family. In this chapter, I'll give you a few important tips on how you can add a unique zing to your product to make your customers extremely happy.

COLLECT UNIQUE INSIGHTS

As you build your product and learn more from customers about what they like and what they don't, you may observe insights about your consumer behavior no one has previously discovered. Let me give you an example.

According to Alexandre Dewez's Substack article "Voodoo Games Deep Dive—Another French Unicorn is Born," when Alexandre Yazdi and Laurent Ritter founded Voodoo, a gaming company based out of France, they realized the process of game development was often very time-consuming and did not always guarantee customer adoption. Gaming companies find it hard to build in a lean manner because a part of the core customer experience includes the advanced animation graphics built on the graphical user interface. Voodoo spent its first three years building two separate games, both of which failed to acquire much adoption from customers. When the founders realized building full-fledged games this way was not feasible, they decided to make their development process leaner by getting their developers to make quick prototypes of their new game ideas every week, which would then be vetted against beta customers. Naturally, game prototypes built this way were poor in quality and often lacked graphical depth, but it was good enough for them to understand if customers found them engaging. When they discovered prototypes that were liked by a majority of their customers, they built on the design and gameplay and then heavily marketed them using clever advertising tactics. With this shift in game-building strategy, Voodoo released its first well-vetted game into the market in 2016, Paper. io, which instantly became a hit in the gaming market.

Seeing their successful releases pile on, game developers started approaching the company to learn how it released one successful game after another. Voodoo saw this as the perfect opportunity to extend its business to become a game publisher, a company that helps game developers publish their games into the app store. Voodoo collaborated with game developers, helping them use the same lean strategies to build and improve upon their games, and then became the natural publisher for the game once it had been fully vetted for the market's approval. Moreover, Voodoo also monetized the high potential games using their advertising strategies, which produced more hits. When game developers observed games published through Voodoo had a high success rate, more and more of them flocked to the company to publish their games, helping the company scale substantially. According to CBInsights, in July 2020, Voodoo was valued at $1.4 Billion, making it one of a handful of French companies to attain a unicorn status in 2020. The company now earns over 60 percent of its revenue from game publishing.

Gaining unique insights through building your product and learning from customer behavior can help you formulate a set of trade secrets that will make you stand out in front of your competition. Observe the unique strengths of your startup and determine how you can work toward leveraging them to help your startup grow. Your competitors can often see what your product has to offer on the outside, but very few will be able to decipher the unique insights you have gained from iteratively building and testing your product. Additionally, your faith in your product will be strengthened with the insights you gain, motivating you further to fill that gap you believe has not been filled yet.

BUILD TO DELIGHT
According to a 2013 interview on PandoDaily between Sarah Lacy and Airbnb CEO Brian Chesky, when Chesky was building Airbnb, his mentor Paul Graham, the cofounder of popular accelerator Y Combinator, gave him an essential

piece of advice: "Build something 100 people love rather than something one million people kind of like," he said. As a first-time founder, you will intend to go for the numbers. More logins, more sign-ups, more active users, and the list will go on. As your startup grows, these metrics will become particularly important, especially to convince your investors your business idea is the one they've been waiting for.

But when you are just starting, you should aim to leave even your first few customers delighted with the product. The customer experience should be note-worthy to the people using it. It should make your customers so excited they want to tell their friends and family about it. Word-of-mouth plays a vital role in how your product grows and can truly only be achieved if your customers love your product. One would argue it's the most essential form of marketing and can potentially drive up your product usage rate at no added cost to your business.

Chesky took this advice to heart and used it almost as a requirement while building Airbnb. He has a background in industrial design, so he used his foundation in design to keep an eye out for the overall experience that customers would love when they use Airbnb.

Many examples in this book will tell you that you need to get a simple version of the product out the door to begin testing. This is a great strategy to ensure you keep producing newer versions of your product and are frugal about the resources you spend before validating the market need. But the learning does not simply end with the customers' likes, dislikes, and suggestions.

What would set you apart as a product is to constantly think of the *experience* you provide to your customers. That is, you want your customers to *feel* delighted, special, sophisticated, or valued after using your product. This may not always be an insight that comes directly from customer feedback.

For example, a review of a customer who used Airbnb might say, "The view from the balcony was spectacular, the sheets were of high quality, the private hot tub facing the beach was wonderful, and the kitchen was fully equipped." Based on just the review, it gives evidence that the customer enjoyed staying at the Airbnb. What the customer may not say out loud are the many underlying emotions she felt using the Airbnb, like feeling cared for, feeling pampered, or feeling sophisticated.

Now, suppose you are in the chaotic first phase of startup building. You've just spoken to some of your first few customers, and many of them are suggesting you build a set of features they believe would complete the product. You are excited about the feedback, and you rank the new features you plan to build for your customers in the order of their importance. Once you have collected and organized the feedback, you plan to deliver the top asks in the next version of your product. In all this organizing and implementing, it may become easy to not focus on the overall customer experience. After all, you are building what the customer has requested, right? Not always.

Think of it this way. If you build a feature and it does what it's supposed to, your customer will be satisfied with the product. Is that the experience you are going for—satisfied? Is that good enough?

Unless there is a high market need for your product and the customer has no alternatives, "satisfied" may not be good enough. If you want your customers to be *delighted* with the product, you will need to be mindful about evaluating the overall *experience* of the product as an implicit requirement during each feature's development.

Maybe you do not have the bandwidth to consider the experience in the first few iterations of the product until you are sure you may be close to achieving a product/market fit. That is okay, as long as you plan to enhance the user experience once you have completed the initial implementation.

In an interview with Reid Hoffman on the popular podcast on startups, *Master of Scale*, Brian Chesky explains how he made Airbnb delightful for customers by finding a sweet spot between the five- to eleven-star experience:

> *If you want to build something that's truly viral, you have to create a total mindfuck experience that you tell everyone about. We basically took one part of our product, and we extrapolated what would a five-star experience be. Then we went crazy.*
>
> *So a one-, two-, or three-star experience is when you get to your Airbnb and no one's there. You knock on the door. They don't open. That's a one-star. Maybe it's a three-star if they don't open; you have to wait twenty minutes. If they never show up and you're pissed, and you need to get your money back, that's a one-star experience. You're never using us again. So, a five-star experience is when you knock on the door, they open*

the door, and they let you in. Great! That's not a big deal. You're not going to tell every friend about it. You might say, "I used Airbnb. It worked."

So we thought, "What would a six-star experience be?" A six-star experience would be where you knock on the door, the host opens. "Hey, I'm Reid. Welcome to my house." You're the host in this case. You would show them around. On the table would be a welcome gift. It would be a bottle of wine, maybe some candy. You'd open the fridge. There's water. You go to the bathroom; there are toiletries. The whole thing is great. That's a six-star experience. You'd say, "Wow, I love this more than a hotel. I'm definitely going to use Airbnb again. It worked better than I expected."

What's a seven-star experience? You knock on the door. Reid Hoffman opens. Get in. "Welcome. Here's my full kitchen. I know you like surfing; there's a surfboard waiting for you. I've booked lessons for you. It's going to be an amazing experience. By the way, here's my car. You can use my car. I also want to surprise you. There's this best restaurant in the city of San Francisco. I got you a table there." You're like, "Whoa. This is way bInd."

... So what would a ten-star check-in be? A ten-star check-in would be the Beatles check-in. In 1964, I'd get off the plane, and there'd be five thousand high school kids cheering my name with cars welcoming me to the country. I'd get to the front yard of your house, and there'd be a press conference for me, and it would be just a mindfuck experience. So, what would *an eleven-star experience be? I would show up at the airport, and you'd be there with Elon Musk, and you're saying, "You're going to space."*

The point of the process is that maybe nine, ten, eleven are not feasible. But if you go through the crazy exercise, keep going. There's some sweet spot between "They showed up" and "They opened the door, and I went to space." That's the sweet spot. You have to almost design the extreme to come backward. Suddenly, doesn't knowing my preferences and having a surfboard in the house seem not crazy and reasonable? It's actually kind of crazy logistically, but this is the kind of stuff that creates a great experience."

As he puts it, if you really want to delight your customers, you should aim to find that sweet spot between the five- and eleven-star experience. Brainstorm and create a list of one- to eleven-star experiences for your own product. What would be the absolute best experience you can give to your customers? How can you scale back from there but still make it absolutely delightful?

SPEED MATTERS, BUT KNOW WHEN TO SLOW DOWN

Moving fast is essential in making quick progress as it allows you to test out changes and validate against customers early. Quickly shipping newer versions of the product allows for continuous development, experimentation, and testing, which, in turn, motivates you to keep growing quickly.

Shyp, a now-defunct company founded in 2014 for the on-demand shipment of items, is an example of a company that could have benefited from slowing down. The company provided a service that allowed customers and businesses to take pictures of the items they wanted to ship through Shyp's smartphone app, upon which a courier would come to fetch, pack, and ship the items to the desired destination. Soon after the service was launched, it was a hit. According to a *Forbes* article, "How Shyp Sunk: The Rise And Fall Of An On-Demand Startup," the company even raised $63 million in funding. Kevin Gibbon, the CEO and founder of the company, admits to focusing on scaling too quickly and then eventually running out of capital to keep moving at the same pace. In a LinkedIn post published by Gibbon in March 2018, he shared:

> *The numbers told a story, and I became fixated on that story. Then, things changed. Consumer growth slowed. People close to me and the business began to warn that chasing consumers was the wrong strategy. After all, how often do consumers ship things? I didn't listen.*
>
> *At the time, I approached everything I did as an engineer. Rather than change direction, I tasked the team with expanding geographically and dreaming up innovative features and growth tactics to further penetrate the consumer market. To this day, I'm in awe of the vigor the team possessed in tackling a two-hundred-year-old industry. Growth at all costs is a dangerous trap many startups fall into, mine included.*

While speed is a key characteristic of successful startups of this generation, knowing when to slow down is also important. Slow down for building features that are core to your business. If a core feature of your product breaks, this can greatly diminish customer trust. For example, suppose you're building software that allows fingerprint entry for car owners. If the actual hardware and software work only 50 percent of the time, car manufacturers who will typically only integrate with quality software will be unlikely to collaborate with your business.

Slow down for testing your product, especially the features that have many edge cases and may have a higher tendency to break. Whether these are software-based tests or manually executed tests, make sure your product's different event flows are tested thoroughly before releasing a version.

Slow down for adding to the user experience. As mentioned in the last point, you would need to be mindful of the experience of your product through every stage of building your product. Look for small wins in design that take little extra time to implement. For example, as you spend time building your product, speak to a design expert to get suggestions on how to make the design more appealing, like using round-edged buttons or maintaining a single color theme within the app. Small improvements like these can be achieved with minimal additional efforts but could actually be game-changing for the user experience.

Sometimes, you may need to slow down even as your company is taking off, as we learned from the Shyp story, so ensure you have the funding and resources to handle a surge in traffic.

BE PURPOSE-DRIVEN

According to the 2018 Cone/Porter Novelli survey, "seventy-eight percent of Americans believe companies must do more than just make more money. They must positively impact the society as well." They also concluded, "sixty-six percent would switch from a product they typically buy, to a new product from a purpose-driven company."

"Purpose-driven" companies use their business not just to make sales but also to do good for society. In a 2020 article from *Forbes*, "The Power of Purpose: The Business Case For Purpose," Afdhel Aziz writes, "The Cone/Porter Novelli survey found that 78 percent of consumers would tell others to buy from a purpose-driven company and that 68 percent are more willing to share content with their social networks over that of traditional companies. Seventy-three percent of consumers are also willing to stand up for a purpose-driven brand if it is spoken badly of."

Today's generation is looking for companies with a social impact where they do good for their consumers, their employees, or society in general. Producing sustainable products may be expensive, but you may be surprised at how many of your consumers will be ready to pay the difference.

The same *Forbes* article states, "Nielsen found that two in three consumers will pay more for products and services from brands that are committed to making a positive social impact. IBM Research developed in partnership with the National Retail Federation (NRF), polled nearly 19,000 consumers from twenty-eight countries, across all demographics and generations, from Gen Z to baby boomers (ages eighteen to seventy-three) and found that 'on average, 70 percent of purpose-driven shoppers pay an added premium of 35 percent more per upfront cost for sustainable purchases, such as recycled or eco-friendly goods.'"

Look at the different aspects of your business and determine which parts of it will help you shine from the perspective of today's consumers. Can you use sustainable-only packaging for your products? Can you increase the diversity ratio within your company by employing more women or individuals from minority groups? Can you spread awareness about a social cause?

I do not mean companies should fake their support or take a stance they do not believe in just for the sake of appealing to the masses. Being aware of what consumers of today expect from businesses can motivate you to brainstorm on the different social purposes that you can support.

Green Toys is an example of a company that made sustainability its core mission. Founders Laurie Hyman and Robert von Goeben came up with the ingenious idea to create eco-friendly toys made from 100 percent recyclable plastic, mostly from used milk jugs. In a 2015 interview with Bright Girls Company called "Green Toys; From Her Playroom to Millions of Yours," Laurie Hyman shared her motivation to build the company after realizing she had little idea of how her own kids' toys were made.

Kids, who often put toys in their mouths, may unintentionally come into contact with the unsafe chemicals used to manufacture them. Laurie also realized kids outgrow their toys quickly, which meant a lot of the plastic used to create them was likely valuable only for a short period of time.

On their website, www.greentoys.com, the company shares:

> *Our toys are living proof that milk jugs, just like the ones in your refrigerator and recycling bin, can ultimately end up back in your playroom. This helps close the loop for kids because they can see their own environmental efforts in action.*

In addition to an already great mission, the company also decided to go one step further with their eco-friendliness by manufacturing all their products locally in the US, thus reducing greenhouse gases and energy spent on transportation to manufacture their toys. In the "About Us" section of their website, they proudly share:

> *From our 100 percent recycled materials to our US-based manufacturing, we're raising awareness about sustainability while delivering unquestionably safe products. We believe that the best way to encourage environmental change is through goods people buy and use every day—and in our case, that's children's products.*
>
> *We care about your kids—how they play, what they play with, and what the future holds. We are constantly exploring and innovating to deliver the best products possible for a playful planet for all.*

As of October 20, 2021, they claim to have used 114,236,943 milk jugs to produce their toys.

A sustainability-driven purpose for a startup is not the only way to go. Even if your startup is, say, purely software-based, you can still have a positive social impact by employing individuals from diverse cultural backgrounds and genders or by simply thinking through the ethical implications of your startup if it becomes wildly successful. Being purpose-driven is not mandatory, but it can definitely help you look good in front of your customers.

Bumble, an online dating platform that allows users to discover and connect with individuals having similar interests, is an excellent example of a company that has earned a reputation for creating progressive employment policies for women. As of November 2021, the company boasts a 4.5 rating on "Diversity & Inclusion" on its Glassdoor page. In a 2018 *Forbes* article, "Women Thrive At The Bumble Hive," Erin Spencer Sairam writes:

> *Beyond the brick and mortar and the office perks, Bumble also made it a priority to put into place fairly progressive policies for its employees—which now total over eighty worldwide, with 85 percent being female. To best accommodate working women of Bumble, the office maintains a flexible understanding of work hours and the ability for parents to bring children to the office as needed. Employees are encouraged to bring their "whole self" to work each day, and the company's holistic wellness benefits include reimbursements for*

gym memberships as well as therapy sessions, medita-
tion memberships, or even acupuncture visits.

Now that we've seen the different ways in which you can stand out as a unique product, let's look at the different metrics you should track to learn how your startup is growing.

CHAPTER SUMMARY

You can make your startup stand out by incorporating strategies that would leave your customers delighted, such as:

- Collect unique insights about customer behavior as you test your startup, which could become your trade secrets against the competition.
- Build to delight, not just to satisfy. Consider the five- to eleven-star experience for customers who use your product and attempt to find that sweet spot that would make them rave about your product.
- Speed matters but know when to slow down. Slow down for building features that are core to your business, slow down for testing, and slow down to enhance your product's overall user experience.
- Be purpose-driven. Consumers of today value companies that have a social impact. Some ways to be purpose-driven are to build sustainably, employ individuals from diverse backgrounds, or think through the ethical implications of creating your product.

THE STARTUP MEASUREMENTS

———

"People are not good at expressing their frustration. The best way to listen to the customer is through metrics."

—CHRIS HUGHES, COFOUNDER OF FACEBOOK

When Katrina Lake started her company Stitch Fix, it was because no other online retail store had mixed data with expert opinions to give shoppers personalized styling options to suit their taste and fit. "How can we marry the ease of shopping online with what people want in clothes, which is really about fit and style?" she remarked in a 2018 interview with *Elle* magazine, "How Stitch Fix's CEO Katrina Lake Built A $2 Billion Company," explaining how she saw a lot of people found it quite complicated to choose from the millions of clothing options available online using the existing online retail stores.

Her business was based on the subscription model. The company used advanced data science algorithms to analyze customer data and in-house stylists to determine the styles and fits for new customers. Customers would pay a small monthly subscription fee for this personalized service and, in return, would receive a box of clothing, shoes, and accessories based on their style that they could try out in the convenience of their homes. Whichever items they like, they keep, and whichever they don't, they simply return to the company. Based on what a customer chooses to keep, Stitch Fix would look for other recommendations for her by learning from the other customers who decided to purchase the same items.

To ensure the recommendations were closely tied to real user data, Lake even hired an "algorithms officer" to ensure the company prioritizes its core recommendation and learning algorithms around customer data. As of January 2021, Stitch Fix's valuation was at $10.2 billion, with its growth trajectory looking increasingly promising.

To create a success of this scale, it was primarily data that enabled Stitch Fix to learn exactly what their customers wanted from the service. Similarly, the relationship between the business and the consumer in every business needs to work bidirectionally, like a fine balance. Your customers should see value in purchasing your product, and your business should see monetary value from customers, to be able to survive, thrive, and continue serving the customers. As your business grows and needs funding to keep growing, the value your company brings in will empower you to acquire the funding you seek from investors.

How can you determine value? Value can be expressed in multiple ways. When a customer writes a stellar review for your product, that's a value that is expressed in words. This type of value cannot be studied by aggregation very easily. You will need to use machine learning and artificial intelligence tools to extract specific insights from it. On the other hand, value can also be measured numerically, through aggregation, in the form of metrics. When these metrics are then modeled on graphs, you can view your company's health and infer insights by observing the trends.

The metrics that enable businesses to learn valuable insights about the performance of their business are referred to as key performance indicators (KPIs). There are some common, widely used KPIs all businesses must track to understand how the company is doing in terms of money.

It is possible you will not have enough data to track each metric for the initial months of your business while you are still bootstrapping. It is still important to keep track of how much you spend and how much you earn month over month, even if they may seem incomplete in the beginning. As your business grows, you will be able to make more sense of the collected data to understand the viability of your business.

Getting insights from too many metrics can also be overwhelming due to the sheer amount of data that would need to be analyzed, which, in turn, can cause information fatigue.

That is why, in startups, it is important to identify a few of the most relevant KPIs that can be tracked closely to observe and determine growth.

In this chapter, I'll discuss the different metrics and KPIs that can be analyzed to infer the value your product brings to customers, your business, and your investors. Let's dive right in!

1. CUSTOMER ACQUISITION COST (CAC)

Your customer acquisition cost is the amount of money you will pay to acquire a single customer.

Why is this metric important?

Your customer acquisition cost, when paired with lifetime value (discussed later) is an indicator of whether the amount you have spent in acquiring new customers is actually adding value to your business.

How do you calculate it?

The simplest way to calculate your CAC is as follows:

$$\text{Customer Acquisition Cost (CAC)} = \frac{\text{Marketing and Sales Costs} + \text{Costs of Professional Services Hired}}{\text{Number of New Customers}}$$

Your CAC will indicate how much, on average, you are spending to acquire new customers. You should aim to bring this number down since it is cash out.

To create marketing campaign content, you may need to hire professional services. You may need to hire a publicity team or social media influencers to give your product a shoutout.

All the costs incurred specifically for acquiring customers can be added to the numerator.

Let's work with an example. Suppose my business idea is to create the online version of a dollar store, called eDollar Store. Let's say I spent six months building my website and found ten vendors who plan to sell one hundred different items on it, each priced at $1.99 or less.

Now, to market my website, let's say in a particular month, I spent $3,000 on digital marketing campaigns, $1,000 on getting professionals to create an eye-catching video that displays the product, and another $1,000 on getting top influencers on social media to give the platform a shoutout. At the end of the month, if I observed five hundred new customers have signed up, my customer acquisition cost would be:

$$CAC = \frac{\$3000 + \$1000 + \$1000}{500} = \$10$$

This means I spend $10 to acquire a single, new customer. Over time, as I fine-tuned, if I find cheaper services to create my campaigns for me, or if I find the platforms that bring me the most customers and decide to advertise only on them, this number is likely to drop month over month, which is the goal for tracking CAC.

2. CHURN

Churn indicates the rate at which you lose customers over a period of time. By losing, I mean the customer chooses never to use the product again because they do not find it valuable. Churn is commonly calculated month over month, but some choose to calculate churn every ninety days to avoid confusing it with temporarily inactive users.

Why is this metric important?

Calculating the churn allows founders to understand what percentage of your acquired customers do not add much value to your business. This metric enables a company to know how much of their CAC was effectively wasted. More importantly, it allows a business to understand how much value their product brings to a customer.

If the churn is too high, your startup will need to create and focus on exit surveys and customer interviews to understand why so many choose not to use your product. This will allow you to learn from such feedback so you can make changes to create more value for customers.

How do you calculate it?

$$\text{Churn} = \frac{\text{Number of Customers Who No Longer Use The Product}}{\text{Total Number of Customers}} \times 100$$

For my e-Dollar Store example, if I find fifty out of a total of one thousand customers do not find my product valuable any longer, my churn can be calculated as:

$$\text{Churn} = \frac{50}{1000} \times 100 = 5$$

That is, 5 percent of my customers choose to never log back into my website to buy my product or services. In the initial stages of your startup while you're still learning what works best for your consumers, you may see a lot of churn, maybe even as much as 25 to 30 percent. As you continue to learn from the metrics discussed in this chapter, you should be able to find different ways to reduce churn and get loyal customers.

3. AVERAGE CUSTOMER LIFESPAN

Average customer lifespan, or customer lifespan, is the average number of years a customer uses your product, from the first purchase to the last purchase.

Why is this metric important?

Your customer lifespan is important for you to understand how valuable your product is to customers. If your customers find your product useful or engaging, you will see recurring purchases from them. If, on the other hand, your product was great to use a handful of times but did not add much value to your customer's life, they may never return, which, in turn, will shorten your customer lifespan. It is possible as your churn value changes month over month, the average customer lifespan also changes. Your aim should be to see the average customer lifespan increase over time.

How do you calculate it?

$$\text{Average Customer Lifespan (in months)} = \frac{1}{\text{Churn per month}}$$

For my e-Dollar Store example, if my monthly churn is 5 percent, my average customer lifespan would be:

$$\text{Average Customer Lifespan (in months)} = 1 \times \frac{100}{5} = 20 \text{ months}$$

This means I can expect customers to be loyal to my product for approximately two years. This type of math may not always be accurate because the customers who caused the churn may have a different profile than the ones who chose to stick to the product. Yet, we will use this as an approximation for understanding the lifetime value a customer gets from a customer. If you do have a more accurate way to measure the average customer lifespan, feel free to use that instead.

4. LIFETIME VALUE (LTV)

The lifetime value is a projected value to understand how much value a single customer will bring to your business in terms of money. Your business should aim to increase the lifetime value for a customer to maximize its value from each customer.

Why is this metric important?

Understanding the lifetime value indicates whether the money they have spent on acquiring and retaining a customer is worth the value the customer brings to the business. It also gives a clear picture of whether the business is spending more than it earns, which, if true, is an indicator of whether the business will survive in the long-term.

In the initial phases of a business, it may be hard to determine what the lifetime value is. It could take approximately two years to accurately determine the LTV of a business, sometimes longer.

The amount of time over which LTV should be computed depends on the type of product. For example, suppose you were selling herbal supplements on an e-commerce website like Amazon, and you expect customers would come back to reorder the product after sixty days. In that case, you may need to reevaluate your LTV over twelve or eighteen months. On the other hand, if you were selling dinnerware online, your customers would probably only order once in every six months, which means it would make sense to wait for about two years before you calculate the LTV. In the meantime, it may make sense to research online about the LTV of similar products to get an understanding of the average number of years a user typically uses a product like yours.

How do you calculate it?
There are multiple ways to calculate LTV. As you learn more about your business, you should be able to determine which equation works best for you.

Simple equation

Lifetime Value = Average Revenue Per Customer Per Month x Average Customer Lifespan (in months)

Suppose I have found research online which shows an average customer shops from e-commerce websites for three years before switching to a different website for the same needs.

Let's say for my e-Dollar Store startup, my customers place an order of an average of $20 per month from my website.

In that case, the lifetime value of my customer can be calculated as:

$$\textbf{LTV} = \$20 \times 36 = \$720$$

Based on Churn

$$\textbf{Lifetime Value} = \frac{\text{Average Revenue Per Customer Per Month}}{\text{Monthly Churn}}$$

In this equation, we take churn into consideration to determine the lifespan of a customer. If your monthly churn is about 5 percent, your lifetime value will be:

$$\textbf{Lifetime Value} = \frac{\$20}{0.05} = \$400$$

There are other ways to calculate your LTV, using concepts like your yearly discount rate, gross profit margin, and retention costs. You can easily look these up on the internet if you are interested in getting very accurate in your LTV calculations. A ballpark estimation can be determined by averaging the outcomes of each calculation, which should help you get close to the actual LTV values of your customers.

From the above two equations, suppose the LTV of my e-Dollar Store startup is $500, and say my CAC for each customer is $50. The ratio of my LTV to CAC would be:

$$\text{LTV} : \text{CAC} = \frac{500}{50} = 10$$

The LTV to CAC ratio indicates the health of your business. If the number is less than one, it means your customers are not getting as much value as you are investing in acquiring them.

You may also notice changes to your external environment may cause your LTV to drop or rise. If there is a new competitor in the same space in the market that is capturing a chunk of the market, you may see a drop in your LTV to CAC ratio. Suppose your business gets heavy media coverage about supporting sustainable shipping. In that case, it's likely many conscious customers prefer to shop from your online store, which will increase your LTV to CAC ratio.

Crunching metrics like CAC and LTV regularly is essential as you will be able to determine which changes brought your business more value and which changes caused a drop in value. Additionally, you will be able to project CAC and LTV values that you are targeting in the future as goals and then track them with the actual numbers to see how you are growing.

5. ACTIVE USERS

Active users is a metric that helps a business determine if a target customer is using their product as much as they expect them to.

Why is this metric important?

The active users metric allows a business and its investors to understand how much customers value their products. If a customer keeps coming back for more, it's a sign the business is doing well. A high number of active users indicates customers enjoy the product's quality and would prefer to use your product over your competitors. It also empowers a business to confidently pitch their ideas and products to investors.

How do you calculate it?

Active users are tracked in different ways, most commonly on a daily or monthly basis.

For businesses that should typically expect daily traffic from users, like a language-learning app or a computer game, the metric to track would be daily active users.

For businesses like e-commerce websites or businesses that use subscription models, the expectation would be to have a customer visit the platform at least once every month. For such businesses, monthly active users is a better metric to track.

The number of active users over a period of time can also be used to calculate the percentage of active users.

$$\textbf{Percentage of Active Users} = \frac{\text{Number of Active Users}}{\text{Total Number of Users}} \times 100$$

The metric can be tracked more intelligently by excluding users who have used your product only once or twice.

For my e-Dollar Store example, suppose I see I get seven hundred users revisiting my website per month, and my total number of users is one thousand. My percentage of monthly active users would be 70 percent:

$$\textbf{Percentage of Active Users} = \frac{700}{1000} \times 100$$

6. REVENUE

The revenue your business earns is the amount of money your customers bring to your business.

Why is this metric important?

This metric allows you to understand if customers are willing to pay for the product you provide. Many early stage start-ups which allow customers to pay incrementally or charge customers a low price for the product will see the company's revenue is very small. This is okay in many cases where the expectation is that in the long-term, as the business grows, the revenue generated covers the initial costs accrued for development and marketing.

How do you calculate it?

Traditional equation:

Revenue = Number of Units Sold x Average Price of the Product

Your revenue calculations can also be nontraditional, where your incoming money is from advertisers or from monthly subscribers. Adjust your equation and calculation accordingly.

For my e-Dollar Store, if I sold twenty thousand items in a particular month which had an average cost of $1.50, my revenue for the month would be:

$$\textbf{Revenue} = 20000 \times 1.5 = \$30000$$

If I compare my revenue for the month with my expenditure for the same month, like paying for cloud services, marketing, software developer salaries, shipping costs for items, etc., I should be able to determine whether I have made or lost money in that month.

7. NET BURN RATE

The net burn rate for a business determines how much money the business loses over a particular period, typically calculated month over month.

Why is this metric important?

During the initial phase of any business, the company will incur fixed and variable costs that may be higher than the revenue.

Fixed costs are the costs the business incurs irrespective of the number of customers using the product. For example, if you need space to maintain inventory of the product being sold, physical infrastructure costs can be considered fixed costs.

Variable costs will depend on the usage of your product or service. For example, if you spend $10 in cloud infrastructure for every one thousand new customers using your app, your variable cost per customer will be $10/1,000, which is roughly $0.01. Variable costs also include the money spent on acquiring new customers, which can vary month over month.

Computing the net monthly burn rate allows a business to keep track of how much negative cash flow is incurred per month and is key in determining the runway for the business. We'll discuss runway next. The net burn rate also helps you determine if your business can keep up with spending as much money as it does. When you have investor money to run the business, this is a metric that is also particularly interesting to investors.

How do you calculate it?

Monthly Net Burn Rate = Fixed and Variable Costs Incurred - Revenue Generated

For example, my e-Dollar Store generated $30,000 in revenue in a particular month. In the same month, suppose I pay $15,000 in rent to maintain warehouse space for my goods, $5,000 in my cloud infrastructure and website, and $30,000 in salaries to my warehouse managers and developers, so my monthly net burn rate would be:

Monthly Net Burn Rate = (15000 + 5000 + 30000) - 30000 = $30000

This means my company is spending $30,000 per month to keep the business running.

8. RUNWAY

The runway for your business is the amount of time remaining before you run out of money and need to shut down your business. The term was conceptualized from an airport's runway, where the aim is to take off before the runway has ended.

Why is this metric important?

Needless to say, you will require money to keep your business running. If your business is continuously burning money month over month without generating enough revenue to make up for it, at some point, you will run out of money, and your business will fail.

Your runway is an indicator for you and your investors to know how much time is remaining for your business to take off before it fails. For a typical business, having a runway of twelve to eighteen months is considered preferable.

How do you calculate it?

$$\text{Runway} = \frac{\text{Amount of Cash Remaining}}{\text{Monthly Net Burn Rate}}$$

Runway is commonly expressed in months. To keep this calculation as conservative as possible, calculate it using the current revenue generated by your business but using the projected fixed and variable costs, say, twelve months from now. Calculating the runway this way will give you the worst-case scenario value, that is, the least number of months remaining before your business runs out of money.

9. CAC RECOVERY TIME

CAC recovery is the average amount of time it takes to recover the costs incurred to acquire a new customer.

Why is this metric important?

Your CAC recovery time directly impacts your runway. Hence it will give you an idea of how much time you have before your business runs out of money to continue operating. Suppose your business is one where customers can use your product for free, but you are relying on advertising money to keep your business running. In that case, you want to divide the amount of money you have made from advertisers by the total number of users to determine how much a customer brings into your business in a particular month.

How do you calculate it?

CAC Recovery Time = Number of Months Taken By a Customer to Recover Their CAC

For my e-Dollar Store example, if I pay $100 to acquire a new customer and a customer on average takes one year to buy products worth $100 from my website, then my CAC recovery time is one year.

10. OPERATIONAL METRICS

Tracking customer-centric, operational metrics will help you determine overall customer satisfaction. For customers who find your product useful, their satisfaction largely depends on their experience from using your product. If they find the product brings them a lot of value and works without glitches, customer satisfaction is likely to be high.

Your customer satisfaction metrics will vary depending on the type of product your business sells. In this section, I'll highlight which metrics will be important to track and improve to get high customer satisfaction.

For a software-based product, operational metrics can be reported as latency or error metrics. While these numbers will give you an idea of how user-friendly a customer's experience is, you will need to co-relate these numbers with verbal and written reviews to determine whether lack of interest in the product is why customers do not give it higher reviews.

Why are these metrics important?

It is important for your customers to get an intuitive and frustration-free experience from using your product. Frustrated customers are likely to ditch the product and never return. These key metrics will allow you to ensure you are tracking metrics that speak to the overall satisfaction of your customers.

How do you calculate them?

A company's operational business largely depends on the type of product or service provided by the company. At a high level, some of the operational metrics that can be integrated within a software-based product are:

1. Percentage of users who see errors from using the product
2. Percentage of users who take longer than average to complete a certain flow of events
3. Percentage of users reporting failures or glitches
4. Percentage of users whose app crashed
5. Percentage of users who gave the product one and two stars
6. Percentage of users who report unsatisfactory customer service
7. Amount of time users spend time on each page of your website/application
8. Number of times users visit your product website/application and do not purchase the product

Customer-centric operational metrics must be tracked on a weekly basis to ensure the software experience of your customers is mostly glitch-free. Many companies also add alarms to these metrics to get pinged or paged when they indicate a software failure. Development teams are typically tasked with monitoring customer-centric metrics and fixing issues affecting multiple users.

11. PRODUCT METABOLISM

Your startup's product metabolism determines how quickly your business is releasing new product features for your customers. This metric can be tracked by looking at the release dates of the features you planned to deliver.

Why is this metric important?

Every business needs to be constantly thinking of innovating and creating new avenues of growth. The opportunity to innovate and make the customer experience better with new features is endless. Product metabolism is an indicator of how quickly your company is executing and delivering these new features. It is also a very good indicator for your investors to understand how effectively the company is innovating and shipping improved versions of the product.

How to calculate it?

Product Metabolism = Number of New Features Released To Customers Over A Period Of Time

Depending on the type of business, you can decide how much time you would like to track your product metabolism. For a purely software-based business, this duration can be three to four months.

12. GROSS MARGIN

Gross margin is the profit you are generating from your business.

Why is this metric important?

Without enough of a profit margin, businesses may not generate money in the long-term, which will make investors not prefer to invest in your business. If you know you will require funding from them to keep growing your company, you will need to show them the business is profitable.

How to calculate it?

Your gross margin for a particular period of time is the revenue subtracted by the cost in the same period of time.

Gross Margin = Revenue Generated - Costs Incurred

CONCLUSION

When collecting and observing these metrics, the important thing to keep in mind is math does not lie. You may intuitively *feel* you are on track and doing well, but intuitions can often be wrong. If you have the right data to back you up, it will give you much more confidence about the future of your company.

The metrics detailed in this chapter are not exhaustive. These are the top metrics businesses typically track on a regular basis to understand how they are growing.

As you monitor and attempt to tweak these metrics, you will be able to understand which business plans worked out in your favor and which did not. Over time, you will be able to project how plans that have not yet been tested on customers will impact your metrics and your growth.

Having such insight is very helpful in determining the roadmap for your business since you will be able to predict which new feature or optimization will give your customers the most amount of value. This type of knowledge also puts you in an attractive position to acquire funding because you will be able to pitch your startup to investors with more confidence as you will have the metrics and data back you up. Seeing these metrics also enables your investors to place more trust in you as a startup founder, and in turn, gives them confidence about your business's potential to do well.

CHAPTER SUMMARY

- The metrics that enable a business to learn valuable insights about its performance are referred to as key performance indicators (KPIs).
- There are some common KPIs all businesses track to understand how the company is doing.
- In startups, it is important to identify a few of the most relevant KPIs that can be tracked closely to observe and determine growth.
- When collecting and observing these metrics, the important thing to keep in mind is math does not lie. Having the data to back you up will give you the confidence to continue striving toward the success of your company.

THE STARTUP TEAM

"Everything at a startup gets modeled after
the founders. Whatever the founders do
becomes the culture."

—SAM ALTMAN

Pacing about in his office, Arjun was getting a little impatient
with his engineer. The feature he was working on was due to
be shipped a few days ago, but in their last meeting, he said
he wasn't ready yet. Arjun had promised a handful of initial
customers a demo of the product and was getting worried
he wouldn't have anything to show.

This wasn't the first time this engineer had failed to deliver
on time. He had repeatedly mentioned wanting to thoroughly test the code against all edge cases and wanted to
ensure the code was written well. To Arjun, this was just
wasted effort because their startup did not even have a

single customer yet, so validating the idea as soon as possible was imperative.

> *He would spend two days figuring out whether this is going to break something when we had zero users. It didn't matter whether it breaks or not, just ship early, right? No matter how much we did, he was conditioned to gold-plate it, dotting the i's and crossing the t's. That just did not fit well. No matter how much feedback we gave, we couldn't shift him in that right direction.*

Arjun Sundararajan is the founder and CEO of Zync, an online platform that makes meetings engaging and interactive for its attendees. For a startup that is just taking off, it may be counterintuitive to not build the best version of the MVP. Since it's already minimal in nature, you may be inclined to build a minimal version that is glitch-free. In the initial stages, when seeking validation and feedback from customers is of the utmost importance, speed of execution matters much more than quality. You want new versions of your product to roll out quickly, so you're constantly engaging with customers and showing them how eager you are to please them.

In Arjun's case, the engineer was not happy with being asked to ship code that had not been fully tested. "He started feeling like we were taking engineering too lightly. We had a different idea about it, and so, in the end, it didn't work out," he explained.

Depending on the stage your startup is in, you should aim to hire people who can adapt to working to fulfill the expectations of that stage. Code quality and testing are important, but it's essential to prioritize them relative to the other things on your plate.

A lot of it depends on what stage the company is in. Accordingly, you should change your engineering style and adapt to that stage. If you have a demo tomorrow, don't push code today. Factor in things like, "How many users are there? What are we gaining by making this more gold-plated? What are the chances that this code is going to survive? How critical is it for us to validate the hypothesis that we're currently working on?"

You factor in all of those, and then you make the calls. It doesn't come easy, and I wouldn't expect the engineer who is working on it or a person who is just starting out to be able to do it. But I would expect the person who's guiding them to give them the priority level, and then the engineer should be able to adapt to their style.

It comes with a little bit of experience in startups as well, when you would know whether you're building a feature that is going to be useful, irrespective of which direction you're going to take. But when you know something you are building is a throwaway just to test it for a demo tomorrow, speed is of the essence. So, having that sort of nuance comes with experience but also from good guidance from the executive level people."

For first-time founders, building a team can be challenging, especially because many of them may not have any background in people management. As your startup grows, you will need to execute faster and more efficiently to match with the pace of growth. One of the most common ways to scale efficiently is to hire strong individuals to contribute to it. So, being aware of what to look for and when to look for it while building a team is key to realizing your vision for your product and company. Let's discuss more about building a team.

WHEN SHOULD YOU BUILD A TEAM?

Building a team can seem very exciting, especially after you have received funding. It's also one of the top questions investors ask when you pitch your idea, so it will almost seem like a box that needs to be checked before approaching them. While scaling your business by growing your team can seem adventurous, it may not always be the best strategy forward.

One of the first things you want to evaluate at this stage is whether the founding team has the required skill set to continue growing the company. Assuming you have acquired at least one (or a few) customers at the stage of growing your team, you should decide if the current workload is unmanageable or not within the scope of the collective skill set of the current team.

Suppose you have a software-based business and you have validated your business by hiring freelance developers to build you an MVP. If your team does not have a technical person who can handle designing different features, providing estimates, and suggestions on how tech development can be carried out, the right thing to do for your business is to hire a technical cofounder, that is, someone who can play the role of a chief technology officer (CTO). The same applies to other roles as well. If you are primarily a technical person who can create your own software, you may still need someone nontechnical to help you out with sales and marketing, especially if you are unable to do a good job of it. If you find your reach is limited, and you could benefit from someone who has specialized skills in a certain area, that would be a good time to hire new talent.

On the other hand, if your founding team collectively has the skills required to continue running the business smoothly, it is advised you only hire more people if you cannot handle the workload. Working ten to twelve hours seven days a week may have become second nature to you but remember to sustain a company, you have to not burn out. So, if you find the existing team is constantly burned out because of the amount of work left to be done, it may be the right time to hire more talent.

WHAT TO LOOK FOR IN A CANDIDATE?

When you're in the process of hiring, your aim should be to build a team that shares the same vision for the product and the business as you do. The first few members of your team will essentially be an extension of the founding team. Their collective drive and commitment toward building the product should match the same frequency as the founding team's.

PASSION, COMMITMENT, AND COMPETENCE

Joon Beh, the founder of Hallo, an online marketplace for language learning with over a million students, explains the approach he takes while interviewing a candidate for his startup:

> There are three things I look for in a teammate. The first one is passion: Are you passionate about what we're building? Are you passionate about what you do as an engineer? As an engineer, you should be passionate about building something cool. Number two is: Are you committed? Because starting a company takes a long time. So, if you're here just for a few months, it's not going to work out. Number three is: Are you competent? Are you capable of building something great? We're here to build a billion-dollar company, and it's not going to be easy to do it, right? So, if you're not competent, if you're not capable, it's going to take a long time, or we may not be able to do it.

Without passion, commitment, and competence from each new member, it would be difficult to build a team as driven toward the mission as the founding members are. You want the energy to be high, and you want to work as a unified team attempting to accomplish a goal.

When you interview someone, you want to see them talk about the startup like it's their baby they want to see grow and do well. You want to look for people who show a lot of interest, are passionate about learning, and are open to doing different types of jobs even if it doesn't fit within their job description. Some of these characteristics will be clear during the interviews. Someone who is always learning and curious to know more will likely display that drive in the interviews without even realizing it.

CULTURE FIT

As a startup founder, you have a vision for the company culture that you want to build. Do you want employees to be transparent and open with each other? Are you promoting a culture of constructive criticism? Do you want employees to be friendly and approachable and respect each other's varied opinions? You would need to decide the top values you're looking for in the team you intend to build and keep that at the back of your mind when you interview candidates.

It will be easy to be blown away by someone's resumé, their long list of achievements, and the different Ivy League schools they have graduated from. Unfortunately, if you find them to be arrogant and disrespectful, they are probably not the best fit for your company, even if they have a great track record. Some amount of high headedness may be okay if you can clearly also see they will execute quickly and be a good team player. In any startup, you want to hire people who are excited to execute and help drive the collective motivation and energy of the team up.

Arjun Sundararajan explains how he learned from his previous startup experiences that all founding team members must be aligned on the cultural values before hiring begins.

> *It helps to have an explicit session with your cofounders. You know, like, "Hey, what will we be doing for hiring? What are some of the qualities we should be looking*

for?" I did that with my current team, but it was a lesson learned in hindsight. You need to be very conscious about managing people, and it can't be something you take lightly. Spending time coming up with the culture of your company is important. People do it in several ways by understanding the values they care about. I care about humility. I don't want brilliant assholes in my company. No matter how brilliant they are, I don't care, and I put that in as a thing now, but it came as more of a hindsight for me.

Brainstorm with your cofounders on the kind of culture you want to establish for your startup. What sort of a team do you want to hire? What are the qualities and virtues you value in others? If you value transparency, you should ensure the candidates you hire will be comfortable having open conversations with everyone. Similarly, if you value humility, you want to make sure you do not hire overtly arrogant people. List out the top three or five qualities you are looking for in candidates before you begin interviewing so you can be sure your team will be aligned with the culture you wish to establish within your company.

HOW CAN YOU CONVINCE PEOPLE TO WORK FOR YOU?

As you begin looking for people to join your startup, you will realize a lot of the top talent is concentrated in the big companies that pay the highest salaries. Hiring for startups is not easy because you want to hire capable, competent individuals who are committed and have the skills you're looking for, but you likely do not have as much money as big companies to pay them the same kind of salary.

To hire the best people for your company, sometimes you need to go out there. Tap into your network to find the right candidates. Engage in conversations with them via LinkedIn or through personal referrals. Explain what's exciting about building your product and see how they respond to working with you. Remember, you want to hire people who are excited to build on the startup with you, not anyone willing to do the work. People who agree to work for you just because you know them personally may not be committed to building the product, which may, in turn, divert your focus into convincing them to complete their work. It will be a game of trial and error and may even shift your focus away from purely just building your product. Arjun Vora, the founder of Zira, explains how he did it:

> Number one is identifying the right folks, folks who fill in the skill set we need. The second thing is convincing them. Like, "Hey, Zira is a big thing, and Zira has a lot of potential. Is this a problem space you're passionate about?" We had that going on for us. I know a lot oIompanies that are like... cleaning up data to prepare it for machine learning models. Now, that is a startup by itself, but I could imagine a startup like that finding it difficult to convince people about the passion and the mission behind the startup. We were a little bit luckier in the sense we had a mission that was very easily understandable. It wasn't like, "Oh, what? Hourly workers? I don't understand." People get it very quickly. That worked in our favor a little bit, so we used it. We said, "Look at all these big companies. There is no one really in this space."

The third part is: Are they actually capable of working nights and weekends? Now, that was really tough because sometimes, if you're too good at convincing, you'll convince folks, and they'll be like, "Oh, yes, sure! One hundred percent, let's do this." Then two weeks later, they'll say, "Oh, I'm busy." We relied on them working nights and weekends, which was not easy to do. In my first year of kicking off this startup, I had a baby. So, my wife had to pay quite a big price. She was at home, and I was working on this, so I used to come back home late. So, it took a big toll on her. So that third part was tough. Like how many folks can actually do it?

We figured it out by trial and error. We would say, "Let's do it." Then a lot of them couldn't, and it was not anyone's fault. It was just the path we took, and they had other personal things that were going on that were more important. They couldn't make time, or they realized though they are passionate, they just don't want to give up on their social lives. That is totally fair, right? A lot of people fell through the funnel there, and most of the time, it was very amicable. It was them coming up and saying, "Look, I don't have time, as you've seen. You've been messaging me, and I've not been able to deliver." Sometimes, it wasn't amicable, which was also a lesson learned.

Then when we got the funding, interestingly, all those people who were going the extra mile working nights and weekends apart from their full-time jobs, they all agreed to leave their high-paying jobs to join Zira. So,

one of the things we've been lucky with after raising
money is we already have this decently high-perform-
ing core team that has worked together in the past
during tough times.

There's a lot to take away from Arjun Vora's experience here. To hire a high-performing core team, you have to convince high-performing individuals to join you, and then you go through a process of working with them for some time, understanding if they are committing enough time, and figuring out if they are competent enough to do the job. It's a process where you vet how your newly joined team members are doing. At the time, Arjun was only paying these individuals in the form of company equity, so they weren't making actual money while working for Zira. Despite that, their passion for the mission was evident when many of them were able to put in the extra hours for Zira outside their regular day jobs.

Not everyone who hires is as lucky with getting high-performing individuals to join the team. There will be certain times when you struggle to hire high-performers who are passionate about building your product.

Anukul Veeraraghavan is the cofounder of former companies like Microryza, an online platform for scientists and researchers to get their research projects crowd-funded, and MyUnfold, a website aimed at building a new hiring process for finding work and talent. Anukul also has experience working as a tech lead in other startups. According to Anukul, hiring can be hard, especially for startups. He recounts a particularly bad hire, someone they believed would perform very well as the chief marketing officer after seeing how well he did in his interviews. It eventually did not work out:

> Basically, you find a lot of these people who love to talk, and they're great at interviews and love the idea, but this is an early stage problem. This is not a middle-stage problem when you have enough VC funding to be able to hire people with actual market salaries. It's when you can't offer market salaries, or like anywhere near competitive market salaries. So, when you're working below that range, you may have to hire people who don't have the resumé for it. Because, if they have the resumé for it, why are they working for you? Then there could be some other problem you'll be working with. So, you'll be looking for younger people, or people who are switching careers, or people who are excited and passionate but didn't get the right break to get into the big companies.

> He was that kind of person. He wanted to get into copywriting. He really liked content creation, and he was a smart guy. He used to work for magazines and stuff, and he loved the idea. He thought science was important. He really found it passionate, but my God, he couldn't produce anything! He would produce one piece of content a week. He would occasionally tweet, and he would mostly be excited about all the things we were talking about in meetings. He was a really nice guy, a super nice guy. We had a lot of good times with him. He just couldn't get work done. Being twenty-somethings, we really did not know how to deal with that.

I think the lesson for me was if you are working with under-market rates, you have to be willing to understand what you're getting into—either be willing to coach people, or be willing to take subpar work and work through pushing them on that, or be willing to iterate through some people.

Anukul believes in startups, the founding team and leadership should be ready to coach new team members with patience because it can be hard to hire high-performing individuals directly into startups, especially in the initial stages. If coaching is not a feasible option, they should either be okay with the subpar work produced or be okay with some employee churn before they have a truly high-performing team.

HOW CAN YOU RETAIN YOUR EMPLOYEES?

Once you have successfully hired the best candidates to become a part of your team, your main job as a founder is to retain them. Retaining employees can be hard, especially for first-time founders since they will have little to no experience in people management. There are some tips you can use to keep your high-performing employees satisfied.

LISTEN

Listen to how your employees want to grow in their careers. You can do this by asking them what kind of work they want to do and how they would like to contribute to the startup. Figure out how you can give them the responsibilities they are looking for within the scope of their influence. Knowing you care about their growth and you are trying to give them the projects they want alone can go a long way in making your employees feel valued.

DO NOT MICROMANAGE

Employees, especially the ones who are passionate about the startup, often want their own space and freedom to deliver results to feel like they are growing in their careers. First-time founders who have a lot of control over every single detail of their product until they hire their first employees may find it difficult to give some of that agency away. Many of them may even find it difficult to trust their employees to produce the same stellar results as they do.

If you believe you may have some of the same apprehensions, attempt to hire people who you believe are smarter than you. You may feel comfortable handing over some of the reins to them if you believe they are more capable than you are. On the other hand, it would be wise not to place complete and blind trust in them either. You will have to work to find the right balance by giving them enough freedom to grow, but also be the person they look up to to drive the overall vision and roadmap for your product.

BE FLEXIBLE

In today's digital age, now that we are in the postpandemic era, many employers allow their employees to be flexible with their locations and even their working hours. Remote working has become common, especially for tech companies. As a first-time employer, you would need to be comfortable with giving your employees the flexibility to work whenever they want, wherever they want. As long as they are able to execute work in a timely manner, fulfill the responsibilities of their role, and set the right expectations with leadership, giving employees that type of freedom will also go a long way in retaining them.

GIVE ENOUGH EQUITY

Startups typically incentivize employees by giving them a percentage of their company's share in the form of equity. This is usually done because startups do not have enough capital to pay competitive salaries as compared to the more established companies in the same space.

A January 2020 TechCrunch article, "Deciding how much equity to give your key employees," explains:

> *Equity, typically in the form of stock options, is the currency of the tech and startup worlds. After dividing initial stakes among themselves, founders use it to lure talent and compensate employees for the salary cut that they almost inevitably will take when joining a startup. It helps keep employees motivated with the tantalizing prospect of a big payday when the company is sold or goes public.*

The article suggests there are several online guides available to help founders determine how much equity a startup must give to its employee, but the compensation given to employees depends mainly on their level of seniority at the company:

> *At a company's earliest stages, expect to give a senior engineer as much as 1 percent of a company, the handbook advises, but an experienced business development employee is typically given a .35 percent cut. An engineer coming in at the mid-level can expect .45 percent versus .15 percent for a junior engineer. A junior biz dev person should expect .05 percent, which is the*

same for a junior person coming in as a designer or in marketing.

Employees who receive the equity based on a vesting schedule stay motivated to work hard, as they hope the startup will eventually become successful, and they will reap the benefits of joining a company in its early, initial stages. Sometimes, based on the caliber of the employee and the scope of their role, startups may have to offer a higher equity to keep high-performing employees incentivized. When you make offers to strong candidates you want to hire within your team, make sure they are satisfied with the amount of equity and the overall salary offered to them so they continue to remain incentivized to keep producing high-quality work.

Now that I've given you a picture of when to hire employees, how to hire them, and how to retain them, let's look at the different ways in which you can market your product.

CHAPTER SUMMARY

- Build a team only when the founding members do not have a certain skill set required for building the product or when the workload gets too stressful to manage.
- In interviews with candidates, look for:
  - Passion and commitment toward building the product.
  - Competence. Ensure the candidate will be capable of fulfilling the responsibilities of her role.
  - Culture fit. Ensure the candidate is aligned with the company's values.

- To convince candidates to work for you, you must:
  - Identify candidates with the right skillset in your network.
  - Determine, often by trial and error, if they can stay committed to contributing to your startup.
  - Be willing to coach candidates who start out as junior employees to become high-performers or be willing to iterate through a few employees.

- To retain your high-performing employees:
  - Listen to their needs. Ask them how they want to grow in their careers and give them the right opportunities to make that growth happen.
  - Do not micromanage. Give them the freedom to deliver results in their own space.
  - Give them the flexibility to work from wherever they want, whenever they want. You should only care about whether they are executing well and setting the right expectations with leadership.
  - Compensate them well in terms of equity. Give them a monetary incentive to stay motivated and continue working for you.

THE STARTUP MARKETING

——

"People don't want to buy a quarter-inch drill. They want a quarter-inch hole!"

—THEODORE LEVITT

When Aditya Sharma and his cofounders launched The Souled Store, they wanted to be the first online retail store that sold licensed, official merchandise in India. There were evidently millions of fans of popular books and TV shows like *Harry Potter* and *F.R.I.E.N.D.S* in India, but no well-known retail store with the appropriate licensing sold their official merchandise.

Aditya noticed this huge gap in the market and saw it as the perfect opportunity to be the first to fill the gap. He was also a customer of his own product, so he had a personal connection with the problem. He had been frustrated with having no good avenues to purchase the official merchandise of the books, movies, and TV shows he loved.

Once he had the idea and convinced some of his friends to become his cofounders, it took them six months to set up the online store and another six months to get their first license, which was a Harry Potter license. At the time, they had little idea about marketing effectively. They had merely been taking shots in the dark. Until then, they had only been selling t-shirts and accessories with quirky, funny designs that would appeal to the youth, so it was hard to tell which designs would work and which wouldn't. They knew they wanted to target a certain age group, but it was difficult to take on a more targeted approach when it came to marketing.

As soon as they got their first license, they chose to pair it with some intelligent marketing strategies the popular social media platforms offered to get their brand the attention it deserved:

> We were four founders, but none of us had any background in any of the things we were about to do. We had to learn everything from scratch—right from understanding fabric to understanding the markets. So, when we decided to explore the possible options for marketing, Facebook was competing with Google, and their ROI was really good back then. So, we started understanding how the Facebook algorithm works, how the ads respond, and how it targets different parts of the country, etc.

We actually didn't even do ads for the first six months of our business because we were still figuring things out. As soon as we started ads, and when it coincided with getting Harry Potter, etc., it became very easy to target because Facebook lets you select people who like Harry Potter. So, now that makes my life easy, right? Otherwise, I was just praying because I was like, "Hey, this is a funny t-shirt. If you're funny, then you can buy it." So, the ROI was bad because it was like guessing. Here I know for a fact you like Harry Potter, so my conversions went up.

We still do those ads and Facebook lets you target very deeply. I can say, "Hey, target people who are from this one town, who like Harry Potter." I could even do that. I could target people who like Harry Potter, who are only in the metros, and who are in a certain age group. That made life so easy, and it gave us really good returns.

For us, targeting was easier because our product was very defined. Let's say you have an H&M product. It's very difficult to target because the audience is everyone versus our Harry Potter t-shirt which was meant for a certain group. That's the reason our marketing took off. After that, we've been tracking it very closely. We have an entire team that does the designing, the algorithms, and seeing which ads will work. That's a process that is followed by us on a daily basis.

According to a 2021 article on Mint, "The Souled Store raises ₹75 crore from Elevation Capital," The Souled Store receives about two hundred thousand daily visitors on its website and app, has over three million registered users. The company is now looking to cross ₹1,000 crore ($134 million USD) in gross merchandise value (GMV) by 2025, and investors boast the company "has successfully capitalized on India's pop culture."

Marketing your product is key to increasing sales. You may be thinking, "But the quality of my products are superior. I believe they should sell themselves." Unfortunately, without marketing your product in the right avenues, it is unlikely to get any real traction, no matter how high the quality.

First-time startup founders tend to think of marketing as an expense—money that leaves the table to never return. What they need is a mindset shift. They should understand money spent on marketing, if done correctly, turns out to be an investment and not an expense. Of course, during the learning phase, while experimenting with different marketing strategies, you can expect to lose money on the ineffective ones. With proper knowledge and educated experimentation, the expectation in the long-term is to gain much more than what you put in.

In this chapter, I will explain how to develop effective marketing strategies that will make your target customers flock to you. While it will give you a holistic picture, remember the strategies provided here are not exhaustive. Today, marketing largely revolves around the strategies social media platforms use to connect advertisers (like you) to the right customer segments. As they evolve to generate new ways to put yourself out there, your marketing strategies will also evolve based on the options available to you. Ultimately, it will take a few cycles of trial and error to help you understand which marketing strategies work for your business and which do not.

CREATING AN EFFECTIVE MARKETING STRATEGY

The most effective way to develop a marketing strategy is to think deeply about your own behavior as a consumer to understand how many of your last few purchases came from online recommendations or word-of-mouth. Let me give you the following scenarios:

Scenario 1—Suppose you are scrolling through your Instagram feed. You see an ad for a new kind of gaming console. In the ad, someone of your age and your gender is enjoying playing a fascinating, new game, similar to the games you already own but different in its own, unique way. The video immediately grabs your interest, even though you know this is probably just a cleverly placed ad. "Wouldn't hurt to check it out," you think to yourself as you navigate into their Instagram account.

Scenario 2—You recently bought an electric car and are excited to take it out on your first long-distance trip. Since your hotel is a seven-hour drive away, you want to look up all the charging stations on the way to your hotel just in case your car runs out of battery. You open up a search engine and type, "Electric car charging stations between Seattle and Crater Lake, Oregon." You're about to hit the link that will show you the stops you need to make when a certain link at the top of the first page catches your eye. It says, "Rent portable electric car chargers for $49 per day!" "Hmm, that's interesting. I didn't know portable chargers were a thing," you think. "It would be convenient to rent a charger, so I do not have to plan my journey around these physical charging stations. It wouldn't hurt to check it out," you think to yourself as you click on the link.

Scenario 3—You're watching videos on YouTube about how to lose weight when a particular YouTube thumbnail appears on the right panel. It says, "Lose 10 lb. in thirty days! *No exercise required*!" You've seen videos with such clickbait-y titles before and know it's all false promises. Then you notice the video has three million views. "Wouldn't hurt to check it out," you think to yourself as you open the link to the video.

Scenario 4—You're scrolling through your TikTok and notice an influencer you follow ardently has posted a new video. You're excited and click on the video. As always, her content is excellent, and you're ever so grateful she exists. At the end of the video, she recommends a new video editing app she used, which worked exceptionally well for her. She even offers a discount code the video editing company created just for her fans. Your employer has been asking you to create informative videos for your department, and you've been procrastinating on it because you have no idea how to create a well-edited video. "Wouldn't hurt to check it out," you think to yourself as you click on the link she shared.

Each of the above examples is a result of carefully placed ads that were outcomes of vetted marketing strategies. The companies that created those ads have likely found the right combination of strategies that allows them to maximize the incoming traffic. To understand which strategies you can use for your own product, it's important to understand consumer behavior. Why were those ads shown to you, and what made you click on them?

IT'S NOT ABOUT THE PRODUCT; IT'S ABOUT THE PROBLEM

As a first-time startup founder, your product will be the shiny, new thing in your life that you want to share with everyone. Of course, it's human nature to be proud of the things you have achieved through your hard work. You may even think everyone you share with is equally interested in what you have built and wants to learn more about it. While you're in this mindset, it is easy to think of your product as the thing your customers want, but is it?

Unfortunately, no. It's human nature to care more about yourself and your problems than you would for others. In the same way, your customers are mostly interested in solving their own problems and are looking to make their lives simpler. They do not necessarily care about your product over others. They will choose the product that best fits their needs and interests. In short, they care about whether your product solves *their problem.*

When you create your marketing content, you must remember to position your product as a *solution,* not as the shiny thing everyone needs to pay attention to. Your messaging should center around how your product eases your customer's pain and should be less about its many features.

When you address your customers, you should also be aware of their inherent personality traits. Put yourself in your customers' shoes and determine the different environments in which they are most likely to be open to being sold a product. Think through questions like: How can I feature often in spaces where my target customers commonly visit? How can I build a community around my product? How can I appear as an ideal solution for my customers?

Anirudh Ramanathan, the cofounder of Signadot, a company that builds developer tools for creating multi-service cloud applications, explains how the type of marketing they do differs from the traditional style because of the nature of the product being sold. Anirudh aims to gradually build a community for his product in the open-source space. Open source is a decentralized development model where software developers are encouraged to contribute and collaborate on the code openly, which is then available for them to use and distribute freely:

> *Because of the specific space we are in, open-source is going to be a big challenge for us. So, we want to get the product out into open source. We want to get it out there, build a community around it, and then worry about monetization later. This is very common, especially in the space we are in, which is developer tools.*
>
> *If we were building something else, the considerations are probably different. I know a lot of people who have hired a bunch of sales [representatives]. A friend's company is selling to airlines, and they're building this product that helps them make in-flight payments. They're rolling out across all airlines, and they're very sales-driven. Their contract size is also in the millions, so it makes sense for them to pick and*

*choose these guys, right? They hired sales right after
their seed round. They're still product-driven, but they
hired sales early on.*

Anirudh explains how their company looks at the product
through the eyes of the developers to determine how to
position themselves well. If your customers typically find
the traditional marketing tactics tacky or annoying, you
should consider how to get through to them using strategies that will make them respond well. For Anirudh's
company, their approach was to build a community of
developers around their product first, so their target market is already aware of the product before they begin marketing and monetizing.

TAP INTO THE CUSTOMER'S VALUES AND ASPIRATIONS

Most people are driven by their aspirations, values, and their
sense of belonging within their communities. When a person
signs up for bungee jumping, it is because they want to satisfy that aspiration of the adventurer within them. When a
person chooses to eat healthy snacks, it is because they value
good health. When a person chooses to download a certain
app because all her friends rave about it, it is because she
wants to maintain a sense of belonging with her community.

As a business owner, your marketing strategies should speak
to the underlying emotions of the consumer. You will need to
put yourself in the shoes of your customer. If your business
idea came from a personal connection, this should be easy.
If not, think of how using your product would make them
feel? How does it address their aspirations and values? How
does it make them feel connected to their network?

Anirudh Sharma, the founder of Air-Ink, his innovation where he turned air pollution into ink, explains how he was able to speak to customers like artists and other businesses that valued sustainability:

> *It was very difficult for us to scale as an ink company because as an ink company, we would need to make ink of all colors, right? People come to ink companies for colors. So, for us, we were not competing with ink companies because we were not regular ink. People came to us because of how that ink is made—the sustainability and the story behind it.*
>
> *Black is the most commonly used color in any kind of printing and production. So, wherever black color could be used, people could visualize us being used. Like in art and in fashion, the most commonly used products are black in color. Recently, an automotive company gave us a grant of $50,000 to create a special paint for a black car. Imagine how big a thing that is for automotive companies. These companies are fundamentally polluting the earth, right? So, now they can say something like, "We make cars by using car emissions."*

Anirudh realized early on that Air-Ink cannot be marketed as a generic ink company, so he decided to highlight the core mission of his product, which was to have a social impact by reducing air pollution, as his primary branding while marketing his product. Artists, the fashion industry, and any business that would benefit from manufacturing sustainably had a strong reason to not just use Air-Ink for their products but also proudly spread the word that they did so, which, in turn, gave Air-Ink a lot of free publicity for their business.

MOMENT OF INTENT
An ideal marketing strategy would be to catch a customer when they are looking for the exact type of product your business is selling. When a customer decides to look up a solution to a problem they are facing, that moment is called the "moment of intent."

They *intend* to buy a product that solves the problem, so if your solution is presented to them on a silver platter at that very moment, your consumers are much more likely to click on it. We will address marketing strategies later in this chapter, like search engine marketing (SEM) and search engine optimization (SEO), which aim to position your product exactly when the customer is searching for them.

SEO and SEM are not the only ways to meet a customer in their moment of intent. Lea A. Ellermeier founded REPLI-CATE Dental Technologies, an innovative dental technology company that replaces nonfunctional teeth with anatomically shaped prostheses rather than surgical dental implants. She identified a unique way of being a viable option to her target customers, "adult patients with aesthetic concerns who are not going to be able to wear Invisalign." Her approach was to give orthodontists incentives to recommend her product to patients who fit within her target customer profile. This strategy helped her meet her customers, the patients, at their "moment of intent" when they were ready to get their dental implants.

We were very clear about identifying a specific customer for the product. This is for adult patients with aesthetic concerns who are not going to be able to wear Invisalign. That was our market, and when we went to talk to doctors, that's what we told them.

Early on, we did direct advertising with patients on Google AdWords. We collected leads and sent them down to doctors. If you're feeding a doctor referrals, that's going to get you in good grace. Every doctor wants a patient.

The other thing that was different was every other orthodontic company had reps in the field, knocking on doctor's doors, buying doughnuts for the staff. We couldn't afford any of that. So, I created direct mail advertising campaigns to send people to our website to take a free course that gave them CE credits because every doctor needs to have continuing education credits to maintain their license. I'd say, "Hey, go take this course. You get two free CE credits at the end." The last question in the course was, "Do you want to buy a doctor's kit, get started, and learn how to do lingual orthodontics?"

That was the other piece: there were no books on lingual orthodontics. They don't teach it in school. Lingual means the tongue side of the teeth, the backside of the teeth. So, we wrote a book. I coauthored a book with a doctor on techniques for lingual orthodontics. Practical clinical techniques like, "If you have this situation, do this." Mostly kind of troubleshooting because

they didn't really know. So, we had to take a very holis-
tic approach that was hands-on, like, 'How do you
build for it? How do you talk to patients about it?'"

Lea's unconventional approach was to give the doctors incentives like sending referrals their way and giving them credits to continue their education to keep their doctor's license valid. She even coauthored a book to educate them on the complex techniques they may not have learned in school. By appealing to the doctors, Lea was able to meet a lot of her customers in their moment of intent. Many patients who were recommended the product when they visited their orthodontist trusted their doctors to know what's best for them. Hence they purchased it.

CONVERT THE INFLUENCER
In today's digital age, businesses can target very specific, granular groups of people to market their products. They can filter down on gender, age, location, interests, and even the trends people follow. Being able to filter down to such an extent, businesses are able to reach their identified target customers very easily by simply tweaking parameters on the various advertising tools offered by social media and search platforms.

Even though businesses can avail themselves of the leverage of such superior marketing platforms, consumers of today are bombarded with so many ads on a daily basis they are often overwhelmed and simply choose to ignore most of them. That's why, as a business owner, it is even more essential to create unique and out-of-the-box marketing content that has a high chance of grabbing customers' attention.

One of the ways to capture the attention of your customers would be to communicate with them through the people who they look up to—by getting influencers to market your product. Google defines an influencer as "a person with the ability to influence potential buyers of a product or service by promoting or recommending the items on social media."

Influencers typically have a large following and have the ability to reach thousands of prospective customers. Many of them also prefer to get paid to market a product. If you speak to an influencer to market your product, make sure they also fit within your target customer profile. For example, if you are selling a data analytics service that helps other businesses increase their performance, you should speak to popular entrepreneurs who have a strong social media presence. On the other hand, if you were selling a piece of innovative fitness equipment, you would need to spread the word through an athlete or an influencer who primarily posts content about fitness.

The second thing to look out for would be to target influencers who have a lot of engagement on their primary social media accounts. If an influencer's posts receive many comments from followers, and they actively engage in conversation with many of their followers, that is a sign they have followers that truly look up to them. If, on the other hand, the influencer has little to no engagement from followers on their account, it would be difficult to determine whether the followers fit within the target customer profile. In such cases, it would be wise not to pay for such advertising.

The founding team of The Souled Store also engaged with the popular Indian comedy group, AIB, to spread their brand name to the youth of India, who ardently looked up to these comedians. Aditya Sharma and his team proposed a unique tie-up with the comedians, making a deal with them to sell their own merchandise on the platform:

> *AIB and the other comedians are from the same age group. They saw we were doing cool stuff, so it was easy to convince them because they valued what we were doing. When we started, we were offering selling facilities, like what Amazon does. We were like, "We'll help you. We have a great platform. We'll make the merchandise, and we'll sell it on our platform. You just need to invest money in it and give us the design."*

> *But these guys didn't have a design. They didn't want to put in money. So, I had to tweak my model. I was like, "You just need to tell us what you want in your design. I will create the design, I will manufacture, I will sell, and I will pay you royalties." So, everything then came onto me.*

> *I had to basically change the way the industry works because merchandise wasn't a big deal in India. So, we got a design team in place. We were like, "Okay, we'll take a calculated risk. We'll put in the money ourselves." And that worked out. There was no one ready to do that at that point in time. Then once we did so much, these guys had no reason to say no.*

Aditya and his team created a unique tie-up with the comics, offering to sell their merchandise designed by The Souled Store's design team on their online platform for free. This allowed the comics to pour in their creativity into their merchandise and also gave them much incentive to actively participate in the marketing of The Souled Store products.

Now that we have discussed how you can tweak your marketing messaging by finding the most effective ways to get through to your customers, let's look into the many ways you can market your product through advertising. The following list covers some of the most popular online marketing strategies used by many businesses to market their products. There are also several off-line marketing strategies which I have not covered in this book. For a more exhaustive list, a popular book centered around marketing, *Traction: How Any Startup Can Achieve Explosive Customer Growth* by Gabriel Weinberg, can help you learn more.

It is important to remember finding the right combination of marketing strategies that work for your business will take some experimentation, just like any other phase of your startup. While learning what works well and what doesn't, make small changes, and closely observe how they affect your customer traffic. I'll discuss how you can validate your marketing strategies at the end of this chapter.

MARKETING STRATEGIES
SEARCH ENGINE MARKETING (SEM)
Search engine marketing (SEM) is a paid marketing strategy that businesses use to feature at the top of search engine lists. That is, when you enter a search term on a search engine platform, you will typically see sponsored ads at the top of

the results page which provide an answer to the thing you were searching for. Those sponsored ads are set up using search engine marketing.

Technologies like Google AdWords and Bing Ads allow businesses to select a set of chosen keywords, locations to feature the listing in, and the text to be displayed to the customer for a paid ad. Search engine marketing is often highly effective because the algorithms used by the search engine platforms are superior and deeply analyze the keywords, title, and contents of your listing to make search results for their users highly accurate.

Search engine marketing is used widely by businesses to ensure their products get listed at the top when relevant searches are done. SEM does an excellent job of presenting the product as a solution to the customer's problem at their "moment of intent," when the customer is often ready and willing to pay. If your business sells a product consumers will look up online when they encounter a need, SEM will be a great fit for you.

SEARCH ENGINE OPTIMIZATION (SEO)

Search engine optimization (SEO) can be considered a *skill,* one that empowers businesses to get the online content created for their products to organically rank at the top of search engine pages, also referred to as search engine result pages or SERP. SEO algorithms use the right combination of keywords on the title, URL, content of the website, the organization of the content, the quality of links to other content appearing on the website, and a number of other factors to determine how the website will be ranked.

Becoming an expert at search engine optimization is essentially free but requires a lot of research and experimentation to nail the algorithm perfectly to ensure your listing appears at the top of the results page. SEO can be considered necessary to have an online presence for your brand and to have a stake in the game with your competitors. To be effective with SEO, make sure to research the correct keywords, content, and links so that your target customers take notice of your product.

REFERRAL MARKETING

Referral marketing is when you give your existing, happy customers incentives to send your product's referrals to their friends and family so your business can grow to acquire new customers. This marketing strategy makes use of recommendations and word-of-mouth referrals to grow a business using the networks of existing customers. In this type of marketing, you provide your customer with a referral code and give them some benefits for getting their friends and family to sign up for your product.

Robinhood, one of the most popular financial services companies that allows customers to trade stocks commission-free, has a referral program that incentivizes not just the existing customer to participate but also the new customer participating in the transaction. Robinhood offers free stocks to both the sender and receiver of the referral, up to $500. When all the parties involved have a reason to participate in the program, the chances of the referral program becoming a success are much higher.

CONTENT MARKETING

Content marketing is when businesses create relevant content to help boost the online traffic directed toward the product. Content marketing is typically used to educate your customers about the importance of your product or to just educate them about a topic closely related to your product. Content marketing can be in any form—videos, blog posts, podcasts, etc.

Content marketing does not only have to be content generated by the business. Businesses today are creatively using content created by their happy customers to promote their brand, with the use of hashtags and shareable links that display a snapshot of the customers' "progress" after using the product.

YouTube is a popular platform where startup founders and marketers promote their business by creating relevant and interesting video content to ultimately get customers interested in the product. Jose 'Caya' Cayasso, the CEO and founder of Slidebean, a company that helps startup founders build effective pitch decks for pitching to investors, promotes his business by creating eye-catching and interesting content on YouTube about investors, creating pitch decks, and marketing strategies for startups.

In a 2020 YouTube video posted by the CEO, "How we made $2.5MM from YouTube and Google," he claims, "Our website gets around 250,000 organic visits per month. I'm excluding all paid and all social media traffic from that number. These are visits to our website that came from somebody looking for an answer in Google and stumbling upon our content. Also, our YouTube channel is now getting close to five hundred thousand monthly organic views. Since we started both of these efforts, the traffic driven to our products and to our websites has generated over $2.5 million in sales!"

Just by looking through Slidebean's YouTube channel, I can see they spend a considerable amount of time in creating quality content that would garner a lot of views by interested consumers.

SOCIAL MEDIA MARKETING

Social media advertising is when you pay social media platforms to promote your marketing content to your target audience. Platforms like Instagram and Facebook will allow you to pay them to select a target market and enter a link to redirect consumer traffic. According to a study done by Statista called "Social media advertising spending in the United States from 2019 to 2021," "In 2021, social media advertising spending in the United States was projected to amount to 47.9 billion US dollars, out of over 198 billion total online media advertising spending forecast for that year."

Social media marketing can be effective if you have a good idea about your target customers and know they are likely to click on and purchase your product while browsing through their social media feeds. The target profile you created in the "business model" chapter can be used initially to begin your marketing on these platforms. Some of these platforms will promote your content for as little as $5 and allow you to pay more to maximize your reach.

Several companies highlighted in this book have used social media advertising to widen their customer reach—Hallo, the language-learning platform for non-native English speakers, The Souled Store, the online platform to purchase official merchandise, and Tarrakki, the online wealth management platform, all used social media platforms like Facebook and Instagram to promote their products.

DIGITAL PR MARKETING

When you pay popular blogging websites, online magazines, or influencers to market your product for you, that's digital PR marketing. This type of marketing can be very effective if many of your target customers regularly read, watch, or listen to content from a single well-known source or person. For example, if I create a product that would make the lives of software developers much simpler, I will want to advertise it on websites where developers are likely to visit often.

Sometimes, this type of marketing may not always require you to pay an entity. You can simply give them the experience of the product so they can decide if they want to market it on their platform for you. To give you an example, if my product is a new AI-based app that auto-detects which local attractions you should visit next when you're on a trip, I can work with an influencer, get them to experience the product, and request them to only advertise it if they find it effective. This type of marketing is also referred to as earned media marketing.

As new online tools and technologies emerge, so do new marketing tactics. The world of digital marketing is ever-evolving, and if done well, can be extremely rewarding and inexpensive for your business. As you reach a stage in your startup where you are ready to market your product, spend some time researching marketing strategies you can use and the ones that seem to work well for your competitors or other businesses in your space.

TESTING YOUR MARKETING STRATEGIES

There are so many ways to market your product, but how will you know which ones are effective?

The only way to understand how the money and time you spend in marketing your product converts into actual sales is by extensively measuring how each campaign is doing.

With every new strategy you implement, you may be taking on variable costs for your business. Consequently, if you do not measure how it impacts your sales, you may not realize if a majority of your sales come from organic avenues or the cheaper marketing strategies. You may end up spending more on marketing strategies that do not generate enough returns.

Many online marketing platforms provide automated mechanisms to track your traffic. You can create a unique link for each marketing campaign and monitor the metrics to determine how each of them did. Google Analytics and Google's URL-building tools provide easy ways to set this up. Google Analytics also allows you to monitor the breakdown of percentages of traffic for each source.

Additionally, you can also directly ask your users by cleverly placing "How did you hear about us?" boxes on your website with options like "Through a friend," "YouTube," "Google," and so on. Placement of the box is important because you ideally want your marketing campaigns to tell you which campaigns brought actual value to your business.

If your product requires customers to make purchases after signing up, you can include the box of "How did you hear about us?" right after the user has clicked on the "Sign up" button. If you do not expect the user to create an account but simply make purchases on the website, you can include this box right after a customer has made a purchase—that is, on the confirmation page of the customer's order.

Now that you know how to position your business' marketing messaging, which marketing tactics you can use, and how to measure how they're performing, it's all about experimentation. Businesses typically focus on two to three strategies at a time to give their campaigns enough bake time and monitor the traffic variances.

In today's age, it is easy to market for free without paying for any platform. Free marketing alone may be ineffective since many other similar businesses will use the same tactics. That's why it would be beneficial to determine a combination of free and paid strategies that work well for your business.

CHAPTER SUMMARY

- Your business' marketing messaging should speak to the inherent human nature of your target customers. Here are a few ways to do so:
    - Center your marketing messaging around your customer's problem and not around your product.

- Speak to the customer's values and aspirations. Your marketing strategies should address the underlying emotions of your customers. Does your product make them feel adventurous? Does your product inspire them to accomplish a goal?
- Catch the customer at their "moment of intent." Be present when the customer is looking to fulfill a requirement your product can help them with.
- Speak through the influencers. Customers will often follow recommendations from the people who inspire them. If you appeal to the influencers, that is likely to help you gain more traction.

- Online marketing tactics you can use (nonexhaustive):
  - Search engine marketing—Displaying ads on search engine platforms to catch customers at their "moment of intent."
  - Search engine optimization—The unique skill of making changes to your website's contents, title, and URL to appear organically in keyword-based search results on search engine platforms.
  - Referral marketing—Giving your existing customers an incentive to bring in more customers.
  - Content marketing—Creating unique, interesting content for your social media accounts to appeal to your target market.
  - Social media marketing—Paying the various social media platforms to display your ads selectively to your target market.
  - Digital PR marketing—Paying popular blogging websites, online magazines, or influencers to market your product for you.

THE STARTUP NETWORK—INVESTORS, ADVISORS, AND ACCELERATORS

"The investor of today does not profit from yesterday's growth."

—WARREN BUFFET

Arjun and his cofounder walked into the investor meeting with a bit of nervousness. It was their very first time meeting with an investor, and they had no idea of what to expect. Being engineers first and then UX designers, their idea of what investors looked for was purely theoretical. They were confident about their business model and their overall vision, so they decided to test the waters before they had built a working MVP. After all, what could possibly go wrong?

> *We painted a big vision. We were like, "In the future, we'll build a marketplace. So, anyone who wants a job can just open the app, and there will be this marketplace, and all of our Zira businesses will be on it."*

I've mentioned Zira in the book before, but here's a quick one-liner about what Zira does. Zira is an online workforce management platform for hourly workers and their employers. The platform can be used for all types of hourly workers, from restaurant employees to construction contractors, and achieving that scale using the marketplace model was Arjun and his cofounder's vision for the product.

> *The investor was like, "This smacks of founder arrogance. You do not have anything of use today, and you are painting this vision of how you're going to have a marketplace and capture 80 percent of the market."*

Arjun chuckled. The investor's reaction had surely come as a surprise to them. The meeting wasn't going as expected, but they learned a lot about what investors looked for. He went on:

> *She was absolutely right! She told us, "There are three things investors look for: Do you have the team? Do you have the tech? Do you have a few customers using it?" We took that to heart. That's when we learned that when we check these three boxes is when we will be ready."*

The meeting with the investor was an eye-opener to them. Getting funding was not going to be easy—but at least they knew what had to be done. They decided to meet every requirement before they stepped into another investor meeting.

So, we had that first bad meeting when we had just started building. We didn't have much. We had no customers. We didn't have a team. At that time, it was only me. Then six months later, we had all of it.

It doesn't have to be perfect. We had a product that was half-built by an Indian team, half by us. It was still our code, obviously. We had just hired them. By the time we were pitching next, we had eight customers who were using Zira, and we had a team, all part-time. It wasn't perfect, but within six months, we did all of that. In fact, I would say even that bad meeting was very good. We were happy because we were like, "Now we know exactly what we need to do before we pitch again." So, it was good.

Many businesses scale with the help of external investments from Angel Investors or Venture Capitalists. I'll explain how they are different from each other later in this chapter. The funding is typically used as capital to add more features, more infrastructure, and more members to the team, all of which will allow the startup to go from a well-vetted product to a well-established and smooth-running business. Since many software-based businesses are easy to set up and can be validated for traction from real customers without requiring a lot of funding, investors also prefer to hear from startups that have some growth to show.

Interested investors will give the business funding in exchange for a percentage of the company's equity. Additionally, since they want to reap the returns from their investments, experienced investors will also mentor the founders, advise them on the direction the company should take, and give the company access to their network so that they can expand their reach.

A startup typically goes through multiple rounds of funding, where each round indicates the company has successfully scaled up by using its previous round of funding effectively and is now ready to acquire more funding to keep growing. To understand how startup investments work and what investors are looking for, let's first take a look at the different stages of funding.

STAGES OF FUNDING

PRE-SEED ROUND

The pre-seed round of funding is often referred to as the friends and family round. This is the round of funding in which founders either put in their own money or receive it from well-wishers like friends or relatives to help them get started. If the startup idea requires more than just a few thousand dollars to get started, founders may also decide to create an online crowdfunding campaign, especially if their idea is one that has the potential to garner a lot of interest and attention from consumers.

In the pre-seed stage, the investors typically just want the startup to do well and may not expect the equity in exchange for the money invested, especially if they are close friends or relatives. In most cases, the investors at this stage are the founders themselves.

This stage of funding enables the founders to set up the initial infrastructure for their company to validate their idea with real customers. This stage includes building the minimal viable product and validating it with beta customers.

SEED ROUND

In the seed funding stage, the startup is looking for more money than just the initial round. Some businesses that need more than a few thousand dollars to set up may also directly attempt to get seed funding and completely skip the pre-seed round.

According to Investopedia and First Round Investors, seed rounds typically range anywhere from $10,000 up to $4 million, depending on the type of business and the funding requirements. From the seed round onward, founders exchange funding for some equity stake in the company, which can range from 5 percent to 25 percent.

Angel investors, who are independent investors looking for unique and innovative ideas in their early stages, play a big role in the seed rounds. Angel investors are often former startup founders themselves, who achieved considerable success and made sizable returns from their startups and are now looking to invest in risky, young startups that have potential. Investors in the seed rounds also prefer to be closely involved with the startup's roadmap, team building, and strategic decisions.

At this stage, founders have typically validated their idea and have a list of interested beta customers who are willing to purchase the product. It was in this round Arjun met the seed round investor who suggested the following basic requirements for founders looking for seed investments.

Is The Founding Team Capable and Committed?

Your founding team says a lot about how your startup is going to do. It's easy for founders to come up with ideas for a startup, but the team should have enough experience and expertise to build and sell the product.

Getting the right founders to build a particular product is often termed as "Founder/Market Fit," where the founding team needs to justify why they are the right people to be building the product. Investors will be wary of funding a business where the founders clearly do not have the skillset or expertise to build and sell the product well. If the execution team has relevant experience in the product space, the right skill set to build the product, and is committed and passionate about building and selling the product, that is the sort of a team investors will be interested in.

Additionally, investors also look for complementary skill sets in the founders. If one of the founders is a technology expert, they may want to see someone within the team who has the potential to manage the sales and marketing of the product.

Janice Riley, the former director of business development at Pathevo, an education and career planning solution uniquely focused on the STEM disciplines, describes her experience with investors when she accompanied her CEO to a forum to pitch their startup:

> *In the midst of a funding round, my CEO and I traveled to New York City to attend a screening session for Keiretsu Forum, a network of angel investors, advisors, and partners. Our goal was to be selected to pitch at the next forum event, which would give us the opportunity to present to over twenty-five chapter members.*

> *During the interview, one of the Keiretsu committee members told us the CEO (a PhD in mechanical engineering, former professor at MIT) had the vision and tech background to lead the development of the software. He was also looking for someone who had the ability to network, connect with the market and handle the business development side of the company.*

> *He assessed quickly that I could accomplish that side of the work, and he expressed interest in investing. I realized then that savvy investors want an execution team. They want a team that can not only develop disruptive technology but also one that can take it to market and make distribution happen. Technology doesn't do any good sitting on the shelf, not being sold or used.*

The execution of the idea is important, but it's also important to know how to sell. Janice's experience demonstrates that investors want to see a well-rounded team that can handle the execution as well as the sales of the product.

Does The Startup Have An MVP?

Ideally, the right time to approach investors is when you have built an initial version of the product as your MVP. If you have something to show that you have validated with your initial customers, that speaks volumes about how much research, thought, and time you have spent in building your product.

Does the Startup Have A Few Initial Interested Customers?

Investors do not want to fund something that does not have the potential to give them a return on their investment. They would want to understand if the founders have connected with actual customers in their target market and have a small set of initial interested customers who are willing to purchase the product. If your startup idea has potential, you will be able to easily find a few customers who are eagerly waiting to use your product and have agreed to help you improve upon it. Ideally, you want to approach investors when you have validated your idea with an MVP and have at least a handful of interested customers who are using and testing your product.

SERIES A ROUND

A company seeks its series A round of funding when it has an established product that is loved by its customers and wants to achieve growth in terms of expanding to newer locations, growing the team, and learning how to monetize the business to become profitable. In this round, the investors are looking for businesses with a solid business model, which will help them strategically achieve growth and scale.

Venture capitalists are commonly involved in this round of funding. According to an article on Investopedia, "Series A, B, C Funding: How It Works," the series A round typically raises between $2 million and $15 million for the company. Companies at this stage are valued at around $23 million.

SERIES B ROUND

When a startup has achieved growth, has a large user base, and a well-functioning team that is working toward further growth, the founding team as well as the investors may want to expand the market reach more. This happens by acquiring a larger round of funding which can then be invested into sales, marketing, tech support, etc., to grow to a larger scale. When a company reaches this stage, they will typically look for a series B round of funding.

According to the Investopedia article, a company that is ready to seek its series B round is typically valued at $30 million to $60 million, and they intend to raise approximately $33 million in this round. The investors at this stage are venture capitalists, and angel investors may continue to play a small role. There can be more than one venture capitalist involved, with one "anchor" VC leading the round.

SERIES C ROUND

Companies seeking their series C round of funding are typically already successful. They capture a majority of the market for their product and are ready to expand toward building a wider range of products and offerings to its customers. They may even want to acquire smaller companies that will help them expand their reach. Companies that reach the series C stage have already shown unprecedented success and have a business model that is continually bringing in further growth.

According to an article on Fundz, "Series A, B, C Funding: Averages, Investors, Valuations," companies at this stage are typically valued at around $68 million or more and seek funding of about $52 million to $59 million. In the series C round, companies typically prepare for an exit strategy, which we'll look at next. The series C round is considered the first of "later-stage" investing rounds. They can continue to raise further rounds as they continue to scale, such as the series D, series E, series F, series G, series H, and so on.

EXIT

When a startup has become very successful and is functioning less like a startup and more like a well-established company, they may look for an exit strategy.

You can seek an exit for your startup once it has become very successful. That is, when your company regularly produces products that are loved by many of your customers, you see your business has been making profits for a while, and the media wants to frequently interview you, you may be ready to find your exit strategy. An "exit" means your investors get rewarded for investing in your business when it was still young and risky.

There are two ways of exiting, either by selling to one of the bigger companies or by offering shares of your company in the stock market. When you sell your business to a bigger company, the company pays a large sum of money for owning all the equity of the company. When this happens, your investors will typically sell their equity in your company to get paid as per the value of each share they own. You, on the other hand, will sell all your shares for an equivalent dollar amount of the new parent company's shares while you continue to work on the business. The new shares will typically vest according to a vesting schedule so that you continue to remain driven to grow the business.

The other way to exit is to sell your company's shares in the stock market. This is called an "initial public offering" or IPO. If you choose an IPO as your exit, your company will start issuing shares to the public. Your company's shares will appear on the stock market, and the general public will be able to buy and sell shares of your company.

A company typically takes seven to ten years to exit. Until then, the founders are building, validating, selling, and raising rounds of funding to keep scaling the company to make it successful.

PITCHING

Almost as soon as you have your startup idea and have completed some initial research to determine it has potential, you will begin pitching your idea to people around you—your partner, friends, family, and so on. You will also pitch your idea later when you begin to look for investing or need to convince potential customers to become your beta customers. The motivation behind pitching is to convince them the idea is worth putting their time and money into.

Saumya Shah, the founder of Tarrakki, an online wealth management platform based in India, thinks pitching should be something every founder should practice, irrespective of the amount of funding they are looking to raise:

> I feel like whether you need funds or don't need funds, it's very important to start pitching to people. You start seeing loopholes, or you start realizing gaps in your pitch, your business model, and your idea as you pitch. When you pitch to a large set of users, VCs, angel investors, or family, you get many questions. Those questions help you in building your product and give you a clear vision of what you can monetize, the things that are possible, and the things that are not possible. I try to pitch to as many people as possible, even if I don't need the funds.

When you pitch your startup to investors, you will typically prepare a pitch deck. A pitch deck is a presentation that allows you to highlight the key aspects of your startup. In a pitch deck, you will begin with speaking about the problem, explain why you are trying to solve it, bring up the different scenarios and types of people who encounter the problem, talk about competitors in the space and the phase of execution you are at, give a quick demo of the current version of the product you have built, introduce your team, and then ask your investors for a certain amount of funding.

Your pitch needs to be catchy yet informative. It should let your investors know you have done your due diligence by researching the problem space, the competitors, and the viability of your solution. There are multiple resources online on how to create a powerful pitch deck. Spend some time creating and practicing your two-minute, five-minute, and fifteen-minute pitches, so you're always prepared to pitch your idea with confidence in front of investors, at events, or even to a close friend.

UNCONSCIOUS BIAS

In my interviews, I asked my founders about their experience with investors. Having heard multiple accounts about unconscious bias toward minority groups from investors, I was curious to understand, especially from my female founders, how real it was. I was able to determine two things: one, it is definitely real, and two, it takes time, but it's possible to find investors who do not have the bias and will happily fund and support female founders.

Reneta Jenik, the founder of Foodom, the online platform that provides in-home chefs to cook healthy food for busy, working individuals at reasonable rates, explained how it was difficult for her to find people in the room who could relate to her idea and her product:

> A lot of investors are male and older, [and] my target audience is working, busy moms. Not a lot of my customers are investors—although many of them could be accredited, they've never invested before. When it comes to investments, they're very reserved. So, I'm talking to all these investors, and they don't understand.

They express it like, "Is this even a real problem?" Also, these investors are wealthy people. My target customers are not wealthy. They are people that work in tech or other busy professions. I have customers who have hair salons. I have a family in their late twenties with a ten-month-old baby. Those are normal people, you know? So, it's a very different population.

Melanie Aronson, the founder of Panion, a community management platform that helps managers build more privacy, empathy, and meaningful connection into online and off-line communities, shared that many investors claim to support female founders because it looks great on their profiles but do not always actually do. Her experience has been there are some investors who genuinely want to help, and many times, those investors have been men:

> *I realized a lot of people like to talk about how much they love to help underrepresented, female founders. Their actions don't always match that. It's very sexy in PR to say you support these causes. But in the end, I actually see that some people do, but it's usually the people who don't talk about it... the people who just want to help, not the people who like to announce they support female founders.*
>
> *Actually, quite a few people who've announced they support female founders have been the most frustrating people for me to work with as investors. People who just want to help me as Melanie are the ones who have been more supportive. Some of them have been men. A lot of them have been men, to be honest. I don't*

actually see and don't actually think women are more
supportive of female founders than men. I think it's a
mindset of just seeing people for people.

Na'ama Moran, the founder of Cheetah, a wholesale food delivery platform for restaurants and small businesses, explains how women, and possibly people from other minority groups, face this type of bias because they lack representation. She shared a particularly interesting experience where an investor asked her if she should be pitching her idea to the group while she was pregnant. Her overall response to the situation was inspiring, to say the least.

> *You know, I never felt I had this challenge. Having said that, I think it's a much more subtle thing than just saying, "You know VCs are not investing in me because I'm a woman." It's more subtle because the issue is that the majority of the VCs are men, and women communicate differently than men.*
>
> *It's just the way it is. I mean, I don't want to get into evolutionary speculations, but women think, operate, and communicate differently than men. So, the bias is inherent in the fact that it's just a different group. It's not maliciously put in place. It's just the reality of it, you know?*
>
> *It's true for other minorities as well. It's true every time you have a majority versus a minority group. The majority group, whether it's white or men, or Christian or Muslim, or whatever. They have their own set of behaviors that are inherent to the group. Everyone*

who is not of that group has a different type of behavior, and they perceive them differently.

So, the problem is not in the fact you're a woman, and they are men. We will always be different. It's great to be different. That's what makes us attracted to one another, right? The problem is in the fact the majority of the VCs are men, and so they have inherent biases.

It's very evident in pitching, for example—how women pitch to VCs and how men pitch to VCs is incredibly different. There is Harvard Business School research that basically compares the reaction of investors to the exact same pitch told by a man and by a woman. They were saying the woman was not confident, and the one man was incredibly confident. The woman seemed uncertain, and the man spoke with certainty... I don't remember it exactly. So, they just interpret the cues differently because there is the tone of voice, and there is body language.

That definitely has played a role in my experience, but I never personally thought about it too much. I did start thinking about it at one point. When I was pregnant, I started thinking about it. I had an investor telling me I might not be the right person to raise money because I'm pregnant, and investors might be worried about investing in me because I'm pregnant. I was like, "Wow, that shit is real. This is a problem."

Only at that time did I start thinking about it more seriously, and then I was like, "Well, if there are

biases, which there are by nature, how can I leverage
these biases in my favor?" There are also things about
women—how women pitch—that work in your favor,
actually. You know, you can get into people's psyche
or subconscious better if you're a woman. So, I was
trying to leverage those biases in my favor.

In other words, I think we should just accept reality.
We have to work with reality. The reality is there is
a difference between men and women. The reality is
also that, for a certain reason, it has to be anchored
in historical reasons, there are more investors who are
male than female. There are more engineers who are
male than female. So, let's face that this is the reality
and then second, let's not let this reality intimidate
us. We can still do what we want. It might be harder.
So what? You know, everyone has their own journey.
Let's just lead by example.

Na'ama reacts to unconscious biases by looking at them
very practically. The inherent differences between men and
women, or the differences between a majority and a minority
group, will always exist because of cultural and biological
differences. It can be intimidating for the minority groups,
but there will be ways to navigate through the difficulties
intelligently by working with the biases to turn them in your
favor, rather than having them work against you.

Finding supportive investors is also just like any other phase
of your startup. You will need to navigate through the ones
who do not relate to your idea and the ones who may not
be supportive of your capability to execute because of their

inherent biases. This is yet another iterative process of trial and error until you find the right fit. Do keep in mind with every investor, you should be comfortable with the relationship and not feel like you are under pressure to execute a certain way just because your investors say so. Investors who fund you will be around for a long time, so it's important to begin from a place of support and guidance.

BUILDING YOUR NETWORK OF ADVISORS AND EXPERTS

Building a startup can be intense, lonely, and exhausting. First-time founders will often find themselves asking, "Am I doing this right?" even before they get into funding stages. In these early stages, some would consider it essential that founders build themselves a network of advisors, peers, or attend programs called accelerators that guide them and support them in their startup building journey. Let's look at three ways in which a first-time founder can find support.

ADVISORS

Startup advisors are typically startup founders themselves who have the time and resources to support a new startup in its growth phase. First-time founders can seek guidance from advisors for a myriad of different reasons like—learning how to set up accounting and legal departments, learning how to rent out office spaces, learning how to manage capital, and getting access to a wider network of interested investors and markets with the help of the advisors.

There are multiple ways to go about finding advisors. There are multiple websites that provide paid and free services to hire advisors for your startup, like Growth Mentor and

MentorCruise. When looking for an advisor, remember the relationship will be similar to that of a cofounder, where you're primarily looking for compatibility. You also want to look for advisors who have created startups in a similar space, using similar technology, and worked with a similar customer base.

Depending on the stage of your startup, you may have different needs from advisors. When you're looking for an advisor, be transparent about what you expect from them, and verify they have the relevant experience to help you out. Discuss how much time you would like to spend with them each month and how involved you want them to be, so both of you are on the same page about what's required of the relationship. At a high-level, founders look for the following from advisors:

- Dedicated time to brainstorm the roadmap and future strategies for the business.
- Connecting the founders with other advisors and relevant individuals in their network.
- Learning how to grow the team and hire the right talent.
- Logistic or legal issues the company has to deal with that the advisors have previous experience with.
- Learning how to influence the company's culture with the right values.
- Guiding the founder through any knowledge gaps they may have.

Getting an advisor for your startup is not necessary, but it is recommended. If you already have a network of mentors or peers who are able to guide you in your startup journey, you may not need to hire advisors. Alternately, many first-time founders also apply to accelerator programs to get access to a rich network of experienced individuals.

ACCELERATOR PROGRAMS

Accelerators are institutions built to support early stage startups looking for rapid growth by providing them with mentorship, financing, a network of advisors, and an opportunity to meet potential investors within a three-to-six-month period.

Accelerators are similar to going to a school for building startups. Many people in startup circles will tell you getting accepted into a reputed accelerator can be harder than getting into a top business school. According to a 2017 research by Mattermark, the top three accelerators produce nearly 10 percent of all the series A deals in the US.

Typically, there is a "demo day" for each batch at the end of an accelerator program, which is when the founders "graduate." During a demo day, every startup team will pitch its idea to a group of investors. The reputation of an accelerator comes from the number of successful startups that have graduated from there, as well as the profile of investors who work closely with the accelerator.

Apart from the mentorship and the opportunity to meet investors, the alumni network is one of the biggest takeaways. The alumni network enables startup founders to leverage the knowledge, experience, and reach of other successful founders who have graduated from the same accelerator. This, again, is not unlike MBA programs, where many schools provide a rich alumni network to students graduating from the same school.

In return for the advice, mentorship, and other opportunities provided to the startups, accelerators generally ask for a percentage of the company's equity. This can vary from 5 to 12 percent and is determined by the accelerator. Accelerators look at these programs as opportunities to find the best young, high-potential startups to invest in so they can reap the benefits of investing in them at an early stage.

That being said, there are more specific questions about accelerators founders should be aware of.

Who Should Apply to Accelerators?

Accelerators are primarily designed to help first-time founders who have little experience building their own startups and a limited network to guide them in the process. If you are passionate about your startup idea, have committed to building it, and need guidance on how to set up and learn from experienced individuals, accelerators may be for you. Accelerator programs can be helpful when your immediate network cannot offer you a lot of support. On the other hand, if your startup is self-funded and doing well, or if you prefer to keep the size of your startup small without the stress of owing anyone money (as a micro-business), you do not need to apply for accelerator programs.

What Do They Teach?

The most reputed startup accelerators teach their cohort of founders in seminars once a week, allowing each company time to incorporate the lessons learned every week. The programs are designed to use a hands-on approach and expect startups to follow an accelerated growth model during their time in the program.

To help *accelerate* the startup's growth, accelerators may also provide startups with seed funding, enough to ensure the startups do not stress out about making money so they can focus purely on the development. Some accelerators also provide other types of credits, like cloud infrastructure credits up to a specific limit.

Periodic mentorship sessions are also available to allow startups to use the rich network of accelerators and learn from mentors' experiences. Mentors guide startups in honing their skills and help them identify pieces of the business that could break.

Apart from this, accelerators also give access to their network of founders and investors in networking events, which empower the startup founders to network informally, get their questions answered, and get actionable feedback.

What Are Reasons to NOT Join an Accelerator?
If your startup does not require any funding, and is growing and gaining customer traction, joining an accelerator program may not be the wisest decision. Accelerator programs are designed to be very involved and aim to engage the founders in many events and seminars that may make them lose focus from the things that are already working well for them.

Additionally, accelerators are helpful only if the investors they bring in have the necessary experience and funding or if they offer meaningful guidance to the founding team. Since the concept of accelerators has become very popular in the last few years, it may seem like many of them have come up with the sole aim of getting equity in early stage startups without providing any actual benefits to the startups themselves. When applying to an accelerator, ensure that you have researched them thoroughly and know that they will be able to help you out in building and growing your startup.

Investors, advisors, and accelerators are all meant to help a startup succeed in its journey. Apart from these, you may also be able to find meetups, events, and conferences that will help you grow your network and learn from your peers. Some of these connections may happen organically based on the stage of your startup and the type of networking you regularly engage in. Every first-time founder can benefit greatly from building a network of capable individuals and learning from the experiences of advisors, mentors, and investors in their network.

CHAPTER SUMMARY:
- As your startup grows, you may need to acquire funding from investors to keep growing.
- A startup goes through multiple rounds of funding, where each round helps the startup scale toward the next round.
- The different rounds of funding are:
  - Pre-seed: To validate your idea, you will raise money from friends, family, or your own investments.
  - Seed: Once you validate your idea, you will raise money from angel investors and smaller venture capitalists to achieve growth.
  - Series A: Once you have achieved growth, you will raise money to focus on the monetization of your startup.

- Series B: Once your startup successfully brings in enough money, you will raise more money to appeal to a larger user base.
- Series C: Once you have achieved considerable success and growth, you will raise money to prepare for an exit. In some cases, you may continue to raise larger rounds of funding.

- Exit:
    - Once you have achieved considerable success and growth, you want your investors to reap the monetary benefits of investing in your company. This is when you will look for an exit strategy.
    - Exits can happen in two ways, by:
        - Selling your startup to a larger company.
        - Offering your company's shares on the stock market. This is called an initial public offering or IPO.

- From the very first stage of your startup, you will need to learn how to pitch effectively to investors, customers, employees, friends, and family.
- Startup founders will also need to engage with advisors and accelerator programs to grow their network and to learn from the experiences of other experienced individuals.
- Accelerator programs are aimed to help startups grow quickly within three to six months. In return, accelerators take a percentage of the equity of the startup.
- Reputed accelerators aim to connect founders with the right investors and alumni network. Apart from that, they also provide mentorship and guidance to help the startups succeed.

THE STARTUP CATCH— WHAT ARE PEOPLE NOT TELLING YOU

———

People never learn by being told. They have to find out for themselves.

—PAULO COELHO

In my interviews with different founders, I made it a point to ask founders the question, "What are some of the things no one told you before you began on this journey?"

The responses I got were very insightful. I was surprised to find they had more to do with the emotional aspect and less to do with the technical, logical struggles of building a startup. As a founder, your mental and emotional state can deeply impact how you go about building and executing your startup. You will realize, as you go through the journey, being optimistic and mentally prepared for the challenges will help you go a long way.

In this chapter, the compilation of the "catches" the founders I interviewed experienced is aimed to give you awareness of the different things that won't be mentioned in a typical startup book. Let's dive right in!

* * *

THE FOMO EFFECT—ARJUN SUNDARARAJAN

Being in the right mental space is a huge thing. Every now and then, you think, "Oh my god, I'm going without a paycheck, and there are these people who are making like $500,000 a year," or "There's this IPO happening, and somebody is making a ton of money from it." It's like you're constantly in that bubble. For some people, it could motivate them to work harder. For other people, it may be like, "I might as well just go over there and join a big company." So, the mental preparation of saying, "Okay, this is going to be my journey, and I need to set myself a timeline or runway and then to go for it," that type of mindset is very underrated. I didn't think about it too much when I jumped in, but it's very real, that FOMO feeling.

Arjun Sundararajan has founded multiple companies like Zync, AarvaLabs, and Ambit Analytics. His current company is Zync, a platform that allows remote communication between team members and also offers cool features like a daily standup event, interactive games, a digital whiteboard, and so on. Having made the leap himself from a tech employee to a startup founder, he has experienced that FOMO effect all too much.

FOMO is an acronym for the "fear of missing out." As a founder, you will find yourself in a position where your friends and colleagues continue to earn a lot of money in their regular jobs, buy their dream homes, purchase high-end gadgets, and accomplish all that by simply working eight hours a day, five days a week. For you, the journey would look quite different, and it's important for you to know there will be many instances when you hear of your peers and former colleagues doing well for themselves while you are still struggling to set up and gain traction from customers. Before making the leap, you should ask yourself if your personality will be able to deal with the "FOMO." Are you ready to leave those emotions at the door to build your startup?

* * *

ESTABLISH VALUES EARLY ON—ERIC KRYSKI

I never really thought leadership played as much of a role in defining the organization as it does. So, I think people should think about what sort of culture and company they want to build from the beginning. It can change over time, but a lot of it is pretty ingrained at the beginning, which has been surprising to me. Even just thinking about it internally as a founder like, "What do I value?" Because, ultimately, if you are the founder of a company, your values typically are reflected throughout the entire organization.

This is something I learned recently in the last year. I always felt like, "Oh, we can set our mission, and everybody can get together and agree on company culture and core values." At the end of the day, that doesn't really work because you end up creating fake values people don't really subscribe to. It ends up being the values of the founder or the core founders. So, I think acknowledging that is probably better than pretending like, "We're just going to make these altruistic ones."

And nobody's perfect, either. Some of the best founders in the world have negative points about them. Let me give you an example about us. One of the things I really value is transparency. The other one I really value is quality. There are a lot of people who say, "Oh, you know, you've got to move fast and break things," like the famous Facebook mantra. I've never really felt good about that. For me, making money isn't the be-all, end-all. I want to be proud of what I've achieved or attempted to achieve and know I gave it 110 percent. Because even if it fails, at least I can say, "I did a good job." That, to me, is much more important than saying, "I shipped something and made a lot of money, but I wasn't too happy with it," because that leaves you empty inside.

Eric Kryski is the cofounder of Bidali, a company that helps small and large companies accept next-generation online payments to grow their businesses. As a founding member of a startup, you may be tempted to establish cultural values as a part of a joint team task. From Eric's experience, the founding members of the team are the ones who everyone else on the team looks up to. They have the significance and the power to establish values that will be followed by everyone else in the company, so what they believe in plays a big role in how the values are adopted within the company.

Put some thought into the values that resonate the most with your cofounders and you. Do you value transparency, irrespective of the role or level of the employee? Do you value quality over speed or speed over quality? Do you value prioritizing customer complaints about any other work? Writing down and discussing such points is very important to set the values and culture of the company.

Suppose you value quality over speed and establish that as a core value of your company. You now do not have to worry about how an employee would prioritize their work if there was a question of getting a low-quality product out the door sooner. Your established core values will allow you to trust your team to make the right decision, even in your absence. Additionally, you must remember to keep repeating your values to get them ingrained into everyone's minds.

* * *

THE VALUE OF THE ENGINEERING MINDSET
—ERIC KRYSKI

> *The engineering mindset you get from being a software developer, that is, the systems thinking and the logical thinking mindset is highly underrated. Whenever I speak to people who are more on the creative or business side who don't have a software engineering or electrical engineering background, they haven't gone*

through the years of having to think logically about things. I find the people who have done engineering tend to have more of a systems thinking background. So, they will actually question the "why" of something multiple times.

When you're a startup or whenever you're doing anything new, there's a level of uncertainty. If you're inventing something new, it's going to be huge. Tons of uncertainty, right? You have to be comfortable with that and learn to just make some decisions, even if you don't have the right answers. So, the way we, as engineers, look at things in terms of a framework is, "What are our assumptions? What is the supporting evidence for that? What's the downside if we're wrong? And how do we minimize the downside?" which typically is measured in terms of money and time. So, basically: How do we minimize the amount of money and time that goes into figuring out whether we're right or wrong? If we've got supporting data that indicates that, we may be on the right path.

Eric mentioned something I would've never thought of until he mentioned it, probably because I'm an engineer myself. The value of a technical founder on the team is not just about building a strong, technical product. It's also about having someone who can constantly question why things work a certain way. For a team of founders who are mostly nontechnical, there are some things that may seem like they cannot be worked around because it may be complex for them to understand the possible alternatives that can be taken from a technical point of view. An experienced engineer would have, over the years, inculcated the habit of questioning the way things work and will be able to work with the unknowns while optimizing for time and money. This may be a valuable lesson for founders who are building a technical product but do not have a technical cofounder or advisor to work with.

* * *

TRY TO NOT LIE TO YOURSELF—ARJUN VORA

Arjun Vora, the cofounder of Zira, often found himself putting on the salesperson hat when talking to investors, customers, and potential employees. As he would pitch the idea for Zira, he would speak passionately about the features Zira was going to offer—a convenient, go-to app for employers to keep a track of their workforce, giving them ways to incentivize employees to work harder, and a platform for employees to enter their holidays and sick days, and so on.

In the process of selling Zira as the ideal marketplace app, Arjun often found himself swayed by his own pitch and would end up looking at his business from the receiver's point of view:

> *The tough thing I am learning about myself is, on the one hand, I have to be this pied piper who exaggerates things slightly so I can get my team and the investors excited. I cannot go like, "Hey team, we're building something that's only slightly better than something else out there." So, you have to be this big cheerleader for your company. Then, on the other hand, you have to be very pragmatic because, in the end, you may face*

your own downfall if you are not. Balancing the two is tough because while you're cheerleading, you start lying to yourself a little bit as well.

It took Arjun a while to mentally separate the salesperson from the entrepreneur and look at the product from a practical and pragmatic point of view.

* * *

CONVINCING HAPPENS BY ACTUALLY DOING
—ARJUN VORA

When you have a new idea for a startup and you are looking for a team or a cofounder, you can't convince people to join you just by discussing the idea. A much better way to convince would be to actually experiment, research, and show some progress, however little that may be:

Convincing happens by actually doing. You can't just talk to people and convince them. We did a lot of work. We had the entire concept ready, we did user research, and we went around looking for customers with the prototype to many retail shops, theaters, and restaurants.

Then, we presented all of that to our engineer, Xiaochao, to convince him. The proof is in the pudding, right? So, we can't just be like, "Hey, it's such a cool idea." You'd rather be like, "Hey, we have already started doing work. This is what we've discovered."

That's what I've always believed. The best way to convince is by showing success because then everyone wants to jump on board. They'll be like, "Oh wow! Wait, you already did this? Okay, now it makes sense."

When you execute on your idea, you get the chance to walk up to people you want to hire and show them the progress you've made. You get a chance to prove to them the idea is loved, and you're going to continue making progress irrespective of whether they join, but it would be perfect if they wanted to jump on board and help you out.

* * *

YOU CAN'T FORCE-FIT PEOPLE AS TEAM MEMBERS OR INVESTORS—MELANIE ARONSON

I wish I had known you can't force-fit people as team members or investors. I was always nervous, wanting the investors to like me, and sometimes I didn't like them, and that's okay. I don't need to impress people I don't like. If they're not a right fit, I can say no to them because I don't think they're right for my company. At the beginning, I just put so much emotional energy into wanting to fit some box they wanted me to fit in, and now I've kind of flipped it, and I'm feeling more confident to say, "No, you don't understand our mindset or our mission. You're not right for us," and I wish I had kind of had that ability earlier.

... I think it's like friendship. It's like dating. People who don't respect you shouldn't be a part of what you are building and shouldn't be in your life.

Some people believe, "Oh, I mean you just need money, so take what you can get." I don't agree with that. You end up with investors that stress you out, and I'm realizing I don't need that stress. It's not worth the amount of money I would get.

Melanie is the founder of Panion, a data-driven community management platform that helps managers build meaningful connections and empathy into online and off-line communities. Sometimes, investor relationships can become very stressful for the founders of a company. If your investors micromanage how you run things or make you nervous, you should ask yourself if the relationship is worth it. Apart from providing funding, investors are expected to guide you in building a startup. The relationship should work both ways—where both parties mutually respect each other.

From Melanie's experiences, we can learn it's okay to not have to make adjustments you are uncomfortable with just because you really want an investor or cofounder relationship to work. At the end of the day, it is your company, and you should work toward maintaining the relationships that help you stay focused on building and growing your business.

* * *

DON'T GO TOO BROAD—NIKHIL AITHARAJU

In our initial company, we went too broad. We were solving a problem for a lot of different types of customers. It's like, Peloton for yoga, Peloton for a regular workout, Peloton for strength training. That's too broad. Sometimes, at the very beginning, going niche is good because then you can build something custom that these other companies cannot do, and that becomes your competitive advantage.

When you're at a very young startup phase, you should go very niche and solve a problem for a small market, maybe for just one type of customer. Do that really well. That's what Facebook did, right? Facebook solved their problem for colleges, and then they went broad. That's the mistake we made. We went too broad very early on.

Nikhil Aitharaju is the founder of startups like Topic and TintUp. Topic, his latest startup, an AI-driven content creation and search engine optimization platform, was recently acquired by CafeMedia, an ad management service that helps publishers grow their businesses.

In his former startup, Nikhil and his cofounders realized they were trying to solve too many problems using a single solution. They wanted to build features that would work for multiple types of customers, which, in turn, did not give them a clear direction to take when validating their features with the different types of customers. Nikhil suggests startups should begin with building for a niche market that has a specific need for the product before they decide to go broader.

THE STARTUP FAILURE— BOUNCING BACK FROM REJECTIONS

———

"A person who never made a mistake never tried anything new."

—ALBERT EINSTEIN

"Here's one thing I think is true: To be an entrepreneur, you have *got* to have a healthy dose of optimism," said Lea Ellermeier after she shared the story of her company, REPLICATE Dental Technologies which failed to get FDA approval for its dental innovation.

> *You also have got to not be afraid of the chaos and the unknowns, because there are probably 20 percent knowns and 80 percent unknowns. So, you have to ask yourself, "What do I need to know? And when do*

I need to know it?" Because you're never going to be able to see that whole path. You just can't, and some people are extremely uncomfortable with that concept.

Failure and rejection are a part of every startup. You will face rejections from customers, rejections from investors, and rejections from prospective team members you were hoping to hire for your company. For a founder who was mostly successful at school and as an employee of multiple well-established companies, going from being a high performer to someone who gets rejected often may feel very demotivating.

Steve Jobs famously said, "I'm convinced that about half of what separates the successful entrepreneurs from the nonsuccessful ones is pure perseverance." Perseverance is the distinguishing factor, especially when nothing seems to be working.

What I had to understand was—investors don't look at ideas. They look at deals. So, I'm looking at this deal versus that deal, and I might think this idea is slightly better, but this is a better deal.

If the deal is not right for them, as an entrepreneur, you have to be a little willing to let it go and walk away. I would tell myself that wasn't the right money for me.

If you take every rejection and try to pick it apart like, "Oh well, he didn't like me," or, "I should have said this," or, "My slide was bad," or whatever, you'll drive yourself insane. You just have to walk away and say, "That one was not for me."

Lea is the founder of the former company REPLICATE Dental Technologies, which created a disruptive system for replacing nonfunctional teeth with anatomically shaped prostheses instead of using surgical dental implants.

As a founder, you have to be willing to be your harshest critic but also cut yourself some slack when necessary. When you face rejections, you will need to learn how to bounce back every time and get back into the grind, but only after taking away important lessons from your failures.

Remember, failure is a part of everyone's journey. Edison failed multiple times before inventing the light bulb. Lincoln ran for office several times before winning. Even the most successful founders have failed multiple times on their way.

When I wrote this book, many of my friends asked me if I was interviewing only the successful founders or if I was also including the ones who failed. My response was, "It doesn't really matter because even the successful ones have many failures to speak about."

In this chapter, let's look into ways in which founders can shift their mindset in a way they can overcome rejections and bounce back quickly.

DON'T MAKE IT ABOUT YOU

Know when a potential customer, employee, or investor rejects you, it's not because they have a problem with you. They are rejecting the idea because they cannot relate to the idea. Now, that may have to do with how much research-backed data you have to show them before you propose the idea to them. But that doesn't mean the problem you're attempting to solve is not real or that you should give up.

When you get rejected for an idea, you can look at it as a blessing in disguise. You do not want to build and nurture relationships where the other person is not as excited or committed to building the startup as you are.

On the other hand, it's also important to walk into your pitch meetings without expectations. Oftentimes, the expectation of success before you have validated your idea with actual data can be detrimental to your overall motivation toward building upon the idea. If you spend a lot of time thinking about your idea and building it up in your mind, thinking everyone is going to love it, you may tend to ignore some important, clarifying details about it that may deem the idea worthless.

INTERROGATIVE SELF-TALK

Remember to take rejections as learning experiences—a simple, "Okay, that was bad. How can I fix it?" can help you shift your mindset into a positive one. This may be particularly hard, especially if you have spent an extensive amount of time trying to get the product or the pitch right. As you learn to take rejections with some level of optimism, they begin to teach you more about your idea and your product. They can even help you learn about your own behavior.

With every rejection, ask yourself, why? If you make an effort to build the right relationships and truly connect with people, not just walk in, pitch your product, and wait for the checks to come in, the listener would be willing to share the reasons why they didn't buy in and didn't engage.

If you had a particularly bad investor pitch, spend some time analyzing how you can do better next time. Did you speak too fast because you were nervous? Were the blank expressions on your investors' faces demotivating? How could you have responded better? On which slide did the investors seem displeased? Note these down for future meetings.

It is important to be gracious when an investor rejects you. A lot of investors may choose not to fund your product because they could not relate to it or may have a conflict of interest with another company they have invested in. If you take the rejection well, they may be kind enough to connect you with other investors who may be interested in funding your startup.

Additionally, you should spend time studying your sales. Monitor your metrics regularly and brainstorm with your team on how they can be improved. Ask yourself hard questions like: Am I unwilling to see this product has little potential to grow? Are my customers satisfied with what my competitors provide, and will likely not switch over to using my product? Attempt to answer such questions without attaching emotions to them. Try to look at the problem from a third-person perspective. What would an outsider do if they were in your place?

DO ENOUGH RESEARCH

Rejections can also happen if you do not have complete knowledge of the people you are working with. When you walk into a meeting with an investor or a big client, you must spend time researching about them, like learning the industries they typically work with, their education and background, and whether they have previously chosen to work with founders in the same space. If you know they primarily focus on investing in the education industry and your product is in the travel industry, they're probably not going to be interested.

When you prepare your pitch, make notes on how you can relate their previous experience to your startup. When you spend time learning about them, it shows them how interested you are in building and nurturing a relationship, which can then make you seem like a favorable person to place their trust and confidence in.

Apart from this, rejections can also happen when you are not well-informed about your own product. Take a look at your research. Are your sources of information reliable? Have you researched your competition enough? Are there any obvious gaps in your pitch that break the flow for the listener? Put yourself in your listener's shoes and try to listen to the pitch from their point of view. What are some of the questions you think they may have when you are done?

If your sales numbers look favorable, include them in your pitch. If you have a valuable product, you will have customers who are keen to see your product launch and grow. People like to support ventures that have clear support from others.

Use the data to solidify your pitch, to help your listeners see they will get value from supporting you.

PRACTICE

Speaking in front of a crowd is not something that comes naturally to most people. If you are the face of your company, you must practice speaking about your product in front of your friends, family, and anyone who is willing to listen and offer constructive criticism.

Brainstorm with them on how you can improve. How can you sound more convincing? What about your delivery can be improved upon? Did they understand your startup idea? If not, which part confused them? And so on.

Record your own pitch and watch how you deliver. You can learn a lot by just observing yourself. Are you using a lot of filler words like "like," "basically," and "um?" Observe your body language. Do you look confident when you pitch?

Practicing your pitch will help you feel more confident about your product, as you would have gotten enough validation from your friends and family before you begin presenting in front of strangers. It's not unlike preparing for a difficult examination.

SOLIDIFY YOUR HABITS

One of the easiest ways to bounce back from rejection is to become a prisoner of your habits.

If you have a desk and a location where you show up every day, at least five days a week, and have a routine you follow to get your work done, it will be incredibly hard to break out of that cycle, even on days when you feel demotivated.

You may view rejections as a setback, but having a schedule and a fixed work location can enable you to keep the ball rolling, even if it's moving slowly at the moment.

UNWIND

Building your startup can be a long and exhausting journey, so it's important to keep yourself mentally and physically healthy. Check-in with yourself regularly by giving yourself time and resources to unwind and relax, particularly after a stressful time has passed.

I'll end this chapter with another quote from Lea:

> *The biggest piece of advice I would give to any entrepreneur is at the end of the day, you have to grant yourself the grace to not always be right, to make a bad financial decision, to hire the wrong person, and to misspeak in a presentation.*
>
> *You can't hold yourself to this ridiculous idea of perfectionism. You have got to believe, "There's a pattern and a flow here in the universe. I'm going to go where I'm going to flow. If that means I missed this channel, that's okay. I'm just going to keep going in this direction. I'm going to believe if I keep making more good decisions than bad, I'm going to end up in the right place."*

CHAPTER SUMMARY

Here's a quick checklist of things to keep in mind to keep the momentum going when you face a rejection:

- Don't make it about you. Rejections can happen because investors, cofounders, or prospective team members do not connect with the idea as much as you do.

- Use interrogative self-talk. Talk to yourself about the different things that may have gone wrong and use the rejection as an opportunity to learn and do better next time.

- Do enough research. Research your investors, your customers, and even your potential employees. When you research someone, they begin to see you in a favorable light and will place more trust and confidence in you and your idea.

- Make sure your pitch is backed by data from reliable sources. Check your facts. Ensure you have a complete picture of the problem, customers, and your competition.

- Practice your pitch multiple times in front of friends and family. Learn what you can do better from them. Record yourself while you pitch and analyze how you can improve your delivery.

- Solidify your habits. Having a schedule and a fixed work location can empower you to keep working toward your goal.

- Be gracious about rejections from investors. Be sure to take suggestions from them and work on the suggestions to do better next time.

CONCLUSION

———

When I started writing this book, I did not realize how similar the book-writing journey is to a startup journey.

Over the last eighteen months, since the first time I had the idea, I have gone through very similar phases as the ones highlighted in this book. I wrote an initial version, read the opinions of experts, learned the stories of many founders, watched countless interviews, tore down chunks, wrote again, got my book reviewed by "customers," tore down chunks again, fine-tuned, built to delight, jazzed it up, made it more engaging, and here we are.

I've come to the realization the initial phases of startup building are almost like life lessons for anyone attempting a creative endeavor. You can say it teaches you how to perfect your art to create something valuable that appeals to the masses.

Studies show nine out of ten startups fail, but that's a mere statistic. What they fail to tell you is that ten out of ten startups are successful for the founders because it gives them valuable experiences about what *not* to do the next time around.

A majority of the first-time founders I interviewed for this book whose startups didn't work out found their journeys so valuable they are just waiting to get started again with fresh ideas.

As a quick recap, this is what you learned from my book:

1. The Startup Mindset—How to get into the right mindset to begin building your startup.
2. The Startup Ideation—How to find a compelling, well-researched idea you are passionate to build.
3. The Startup Business Model—How to add detail to your idea to thoroughly understand the different cogs in the machine.
4. The Startup Cofounder—How to look for a compatible cofounder who will work with you toward the success of your startup.
5. The Startup Execution—Phase One—How to take small steps toward building the right product by repeatedly validating it with your actual customers.
6. The Startup Evolution—How to build the product your customers actually want by going over the cycle of rewiring and retooling or simply by changing directions.
7. The Startup Jazz—How to build your product so it leaves your customers so delighted they cannot stop raving about it.
8. The Startup Measurements—How to observe key metrics and trends to learn how your startup is doing.
9. The Startup Team—How to build a team that is as passionate as you are about building a valuable product for your customers.
10. The Startup Marketing—How to sell your product like your customers cannot do without it.

11. The Startup Network—How to build effective relationships with investors, advisors, and experts in the field, and learn how to navigate through unconscious biases to come out strong.
12. The Startup Catch—What the founders I interviewed identified as "catches" that no one told them about.
13. The Startup Failure—How to overcome rejection and bounce back quickly so you can keep the ball rolling.

My aim for this book is to guide and inspire people like you and me, employees in regular day jobs, to think beyond the realms of our daily lives and attempt to build something extraordinary. There are multiple ways to get started without making significant changes to your life by just taking baby steps in the right direction. I hope I've convinced you the journey will be worth it, no matter what the outcome turns out to be. Let today be the day you take a step toward launching your own startup.

To create this book, I read multiple books and countless articles on the internet, listened to some fantastic podcasts, and watched many interviews and startup-related videos on YouTube.

If I had to recommend the top books to read from here on, some suggestions are: *The $100 Startup* by Chris Guillebeau, *Founders at Work* by Jessica Livingston, *The Lean Startup* by Eric Ries, and *Jugaad* by Navi Radjou, Jaideep Prabhu, and Simone Ahuja.

Podcasts I would recommend are *Masters of Scale* hosted by Reid Hoffman and *The Tim Ferriss Show* hosted by Timothy Ferris.

For articles to read online, I would highly recommend *Harvard Business Review* and *Forbes* for any startup-related topic you're interested in learning more about.

On YouTube, I found the channels Y Combinator, Slidebean, and Strategyzer to be very useful for learning about founder journeys and creating successful, scalable startups.

If you've come this far in my book, I'm assuming you must have liked what I had to offer. My product seems to have worked its magic on you. Now, it's time to get to work so your product can work its magic on others too.

ABOUT THE FOUNDERS

___

ADITYA SHARMA

Aditya Sharma is the cofounder of The Souled Store, a pop culture and fashion apparel brand born in India. Aditya and his brand have been featured in *Forbes* and other big publications as one of the most capital-efficient businesses in India. He loves exchanging knowledge with fellow entrepreneurs and acts as a mentor in the Indian startup ecosystem. Aditya has also used his brand to advocate for social causes like women's empowerment, mental health awareness, and plastic waste reduction. When he's not working, he enjoys outdoor activities like trekking, biking, and creating music on his handpan.

ANIRUDH RAMANATHAN

Anirudh Ramanathan is cofounder of Signadot, a seed-stage startup in the developer tools space that was funded by Y Combinator. He was previously a software engineer on Kubernetes at Google, where he worked on core components, including Kubernetes controllers and operators. Anirudh is passionate about startup culture and building products that bring simplicity to complex problems. In his spare time, he loves sailing and reading science fiction.

ANIRUDH SHARMA

Anirudh Sharma is an *MIT Technology Review* "35 Under 35 Innovator," *Forbes* "30 Under 30," Awardee, and the founder of Graviky Labs. His company Graviky is addressing the air pollution problem by treating it as a waste-management problem and developing novel materials and leading industry shifts around them. He loves problem-solving and builds novel technologies that have a large social impact and narratives. He uses augmented/mixed reality, art, cybernetics, wearables, and materials to create new impactful concepts that question the conventional way of solving problems. Anirudh graduated from the Fluid Interfaces Group at MIT Media Lab, at Massachusetts Institute of Technology, where he worked on "augmented reality/2D/3D using transparent OLED displays." Prior to the MIT Media Lab, his past venture Ducere made athletic tracking wearable computers embedded within shoes. The shoes were started as a navigation aid for the visually impaired.

ANUKUL VEERARAGHAVAN

Anukul Veeraraghavan is a lead software engineer at Peer-Street. Prior to PeerStreet, he worked as a senior software engineer at Microsoft for five years. Anukul has cofounded several startups like MyUnfold, an automated platform that matches talent to jobs, and Microryza, a platform for researchers to crowd-fund research projects which was aimed to change the way science funding works. He has also worked in several other startups such as Showqase, Quve, and Boomerang Commerce. Anukul graduated from the University of Washington with a bachelor's in mathematics. In his spare time, he loves to cook, play and watch soccer, and volunteer for educational causes.

ARJUN SUNDARARAJAN

Arjun is the cofounder and CEO of Zync, an interactive platform for running engaging virtual events. He is an engineer by training and spent the early days of his career building products for Microsoft and Foursquare. He started his first company in 2016 when he was an entrepreneur in residence at SRI International. His big vision is to use technology to change how we connect and collaborate virtually and make it more meaningful than meeting in person. Outside work, he spends time learning to live life from his toddler and newborn. He also geeks out about social emotional learning and behavioral science on the side.

ARJUN VORA

Arjun Vora is the cofounder of Zira, an employee management platform that has a robust AI at its core that helps predict demand, create schedules, and maintain preferences. Prior to founding Zira, he worked at Uber as the head of design for five years, where he led the design of the driver app. Arjun got his Master of Science in Human-Computer Interaction from Michigan University and his Bachelor of Science in Computer Engineering from Mumbai University. In his spare time, he loves playing with his two-year-old daughter, cooking, and hiking in national parks.

ASHISH ROHIL

Ashish Rohil leads strategy and business operations at Sunrun, the largest residential solar player in the US. He is exploring entrepreneurial opportunities related to FinTech and Climate Tech. Prior to Sunrun, he worked as a consultant at BCG where he worked on strategy, strategic planning, and pricing topics across various industries. He is an MBA graduate from Kellogg. During his MBA, he worked with a search fund and developed an interest in entrepreneurship through acquisition (ETA). Ashish is also the cofounder of the former startup, Madbooks.com, an online platform for the sale and purchase of used books. He is passionate about building consumer brands and growing businesses in emerging markets. In his spare time, he likes to play chess, hike trails, and enjoy nature.

ERIC KRYSKI

Eric Kryski is the cofounder and CEO of Bidali—a financial infrastructure company that uses blockchain technology to provide better, cheaper, and more transparent financial services. He holds a bachelor's degree in computer science from the University of Calgary. Eric has been building software and distributed systems for over fifteen years, has previously spoken during the World Economic Forum about the future of money, and has advised multiple governments on their financial digital transformation strategies. In his spare time, he likes to box, brew beer, play video games, and get outdoors with his family.

HELENA RONIS

Helena Ronis is the cofounder and CEO at AllFactors, a web analytics software for businesses to drive marketing and growth. Helena was born in Ukraine and raised in Israel. She served in the tech unit of the Israeli Air Force. Before starting AllFactors she was a two-time founder and also worked in product and marketing at other companies. Helena also started what became the largest group for women founders called Women Founders Community on Facebook. In her spare time, Helena enjoys advising startups on Go To Market strategy for SaaS, including marketing, sales, product, growth, and metrics.

JOON BEH

Joon Beh is the cofounder and CEO of Hallo, an online marketplace for language learning with over 1M students from around the world. He worked at Deloitte as a consultant in Silicon Valley, helping tech giants such as Uber, Amazon, and LinkedIn. Joon was featured in *Forbes* and nominated as one of the top twenties in their twenties by *Utah Business.* As a Korean immigrant, Joon is fulfilling his American dream and aspiring to empower others to find more opportunities in life through language. In his spare time, he enjoys playing tennis and pickleball, and he spends time learning more about other entrepreneurs to continue learning.

LEA A. ELLERMEIER

Lea Ellermeier is a serial entrepreneur and cofounder of 2C Dental AG, REPLICATE Dental Technologies, and Lingualcare, Inc., a Dallas, Texas-based dental technology company that developed and marketed disruptive technology for mass customization of invisible, orthodontic braces with operations in the US, Germany, and Mexico. Lingualcare won the prestigious Dallas 100 Entrepreneur Award in 2007 for being one of the fastest-growing, most dynamic companies in Dallas. Lingualcare was purchased by 3M Company in November 2007. Lea currently serves as president of Sheep-Medical USA. Lea has a bachelor's in political science (cum laude) from the University of Texas El Paso and an MBA from the Thunderbird School of Global Management in Glendale, Arizona. She is the author of *Finding the Exit; It's Not Where You Start It's Where You Finish* and is a frequent speaker at industry and entrepreneurial events.

LEIGHTON HEALEY

Leighton is a serial entrepreneur, innovator, and community and business leader with over twelve years of experience establishing, launching, and growing successful ventures. In 2020, he founded KnowHow, a platform for equipping teams with the step-by-step processes they need to do their jobs effectively. In 2016, he founded Bootkik, a platform for users to share their expertise with each other. With Bootkik, keynote speakers, teachers, and thought leaders create guides for their audience to implement into their life and work. Leighton's background includes seven years in executive leadership with College Pro, where he was responsible for over forty million dollars in revenue. He got his start in entrepreneurship with the founding of LTX Trades Ltd. in 2005, where he won dozens of awards and set records as one of the most successful franchise owners in College Pro's over forty years of operation.

MELANIE ARONSON

Melanie Aronson is the founder of Panion, an empathy-driven community-building platform that helps creators connect people through common interests and experiences and engages them through events and workshops in their area. She has a background in anthropology, documentary filmmaking, and design, and has been working as a freelance photographer, filmmaker, teacher, and consultant for the last eight years. She has also spent three years working as a sales and personal shopping specialist at Apple in New York City. Melanie has a bachelor's degree in anthropology from Columbia University and a master's degree in documentary filmmaking from the School of Visuals Arts in New York City. She is also a Fulbright recipient. In her spare time, she loves doing yoga, cooking, and traveling.

NA'AMA MORAN

Na'ama Moran is the cofounder and CEO of Cheetah, an e-commerce platform designed for independent restaurants to order wholesale food and supplies. Prior to Cheetah, she founded several startups like Sourcery, a platform that provides food service expertise, easy to use technology, and customer support to professional food businesses, and Zappedy, a services platform enabling local businesses to close the loop between online marketing and off-line sales. Na'ama came to the US from Israel to study economics, math, and political science at Cornell and started her career with Greylock Capital Management as a financial analyst before moving to Silicon Valley to found her startups. In her spare time, Na'ama loves to practice yoga, hike the beautiful Bay Area trails, and read science fiction books.

NIKHIL AITHARAJU

Nikhil is a serial entrepreneur who cofounded and sold two companies. In 2019, he cofounded Topic, an AI content optimization platform that helps marketers create high-quality content at scale. He grew the company to serve hundreds of customers without raising any outside funding. He then successfully sold it to CafeMedia in 2021. Prior to Topic, he cofounded TINT—a visual user-generated content marketing platform. He started the company in his college basement with his cofounders and grew it to five million dollars in annual recurring revenue. TINT was eventually bought by Filestack in 2018. Being an immigrant, he had to navigate the complex immigration system to pursue his American dream. In his free time, he listens to business podcasts and works on DIY projects at home.

RENETA JENIK

Reneta Jenik is the founder and CEO of Foodom (myfoodom.com), everyone's personal chef marketplace. She is on a mission to have in-home chefs for every household and travel rental. She is an AI/ML, product, and operation executive and a former employee of Intel, SanDisk, and several startups. She has experience growing businesses from the ground up to make billions of dollars across different markets. She was born in Ukraine, moved to Israel at the age of three, and later on moved to work in tech in Silicon Valley. Her life experiences shaped her to be a direct, data-driven critical thinker who is passionate about building out-of-the-box solutions for inefficiencies and pain points in huge markets. When she is not working on Foodom, she's outdoorsy and is infected by the triathlons bug. She also loves volunteering with her family in the community, and mentoring peers in her startup circle. Apart from that, she practices mindfulness regularly.

SAUMYA SHAH

Saumya is the founder of Tarrakki, a comprehensive wealth management app that enables customers to strategically invest their money in a variety of asset classes. Saumya moved back to India to launch Tarrakki with the sole aim of providing unbiased investment advisory to Indians by leveraging technology. Before moving back to India to launch Tarrakki, Saumya worked with Deloitte Advisory in New York. He worked with their financial institutions group and advised on multiple mergers and acquisitions transactions, private debt and equity valuations, and purchase price allocations. Saumya has worked across two countries (USA and India) and four sectors (internet, media, infrastructure, and financial institutions). In this spare time, Saumya is an avid fan of football and also enjoys playing golf.

VARUN SHETH

Varun Sheth is the cofounder and CEO of Ketto.org, Asia's largest online crowdfunding platform, which fuels a wide variety of sustainable causes, right from fundraising for startups to fundraising for medical purposes. Varun's journey in the social impact sector began early in his college days. He volunteered with NGOs such as The Akshara Foundation and Care India, and he is also an alumnus of Dasra Social Impact. Today, Varun has successfully steered Ketto to stratospheric heights. This is evident in the several awards and accolades he has received over the years. He was chosen in the 2017

Forbes "30 Under 30 List," 2018 *Fortune* magazine's "40 Under 40 List," and 2019 *Economic Times'* "40 Under 40 List." He has also been invited as a speaker at several coveted speaking events by the Harvard Business School, TEDx, IAS University, IITs, and TISS.

ACKNOWLEDGMENTS

———

First, I would like to thank the founders, whose invaluable experiences helped me create this book. Thank you for your time and for sharing the highs and lows of your journeys with me. Your stories are the reason this book has flavor. They give my readers the opportunity to experience the startup world through your eyes.

To my husband, Gaurav Khedekar, for being the best companion one could ask for. Without your patience, guidance, and encouragement every step of the way, I could not have written this book. Thank you for being the absolute rockstar you are, and thank you for being my sweetest beta reader. I love you.

To my parents, my amma and appa—Padma Shekar and K. N. Shekar—thank you for being the reason I could write this book today. Thank you for bringing me up to continually strive to be the best version of me every day. Your love and support have made me who I am, and I am ever so grateful to have you as my parents. Appa, thank you for reviewing every chapter of my book and giving me your feedback.

To my sister and brother-in-law, Shuba Shekar and Prashant Hegde, thank you for your unconditional love, encouragement, and support in this journey and in every endeavor I take on. You both are awesome, and I'm thankful for you every day.

To my in-laws, my mummy and pappa—Seema and Govind Khedekar—thank you for cheering me on and showing me how proud they are of their daughter-in-law. Thank you for your endless support and for bringing Gaurav up to be the person he is today.

To Anish Ghulati, thank you for being the beta reader with the most insightful suggestions and for agreeing to be my mentor in every goal I take on. Your comments about changing the flow, adding more detail in specific parts, and removing irrelevant content all helped make this book what it is today.

To Aditi Halan, thank you for supporting me on this journey and for introducing me to some of the most interesting founders who were happy to share their experiences with me. You have no idea how many times I've thanked you while writing this book.

To Domenica Mata Rodriguez, thank you for taking the time to review the very first, uncut version of my book. Your detailed comments helped me understand what many of my readers would expect from this book.

To Meghna Kedia, Saagar Chugh, and Manasi Surve, because this may be the only book I write, and if that's the case, I want your names to show up here. Thank you for being my forever homies!

Thank you to my closest cousins and their families, who have always been there for me every time I needed an extra push, a pat on my back, or even just a silly joke to make me laugh.

To Shrilata Murthy, thank you for helping me find the right avenue to make this book happen and for answering the countless questions I had about publishing. I may not have written this book if you hadn't shown me the way.

To my other beta readers, Sachit Muckaden, Nikhil Nambiar, and Divyanshu Bhadoria, thank you for taking the time to review the first few chapters and giving me your valuable suggestions.

To my amazing publishing team at The Creator Institute and New Degree Press for their endless guidance through this journey and for giving me multiple deadlines to keep me motivated—thank you all. I most definitely could not have accomplished this without you: Eric Koester, Janice Riley, Ilia Epifanov, Kristy Carter, Angela Mitchell, Nikola Tikoski, Brian Bies, Venus Bradley, Gjorgji Pejkovski, Simona Gjurovska, Amanda Brown, Vladimir Dudaš, Natalie Bailey, and the rest of the team.

Finally, thank you to my backers, who preordered my book before I had even written it. Thank you for placing your trust in my capability to create a useful book. I am immensely grateful for all of you.

Aishwarya Koos
Ajit Padukone
Akanksh Shetty

Akanksha Potdar
Akshada Dattilo
Akshay Hegiste

Ameya Joshi

Amol Khor

Amruta dhotre

Anand Markande

Anirudh

Anish Ghulati

Antony Issakov

Anuj Trivedi

Apoorva Sawhney

Apurva Limaye

Archanaa Jayaraman

Arjun Vora

Ashwin thombre

Bhargavi Devarajan

Bhavin Patel

Deepa Ratnam

Deepak Mohan

Dimple Nangia

Dishen Mistry

Divya Kinni

Faizan Khatri

Fatema Aurangabadi

Faza Chugtai

Gaurav Khedekar

Govind Khedekar

Harani Mukkala

Harshal Bonde

Ilia Epifanov

Isha Arora

Janhavi Devarajan

Jaydev Hari

Jyotsna Parthasarathy

K N Shekar

Kalid Azad

Kalyani Patil

Karan Chimedia

Kaushal Ambani

Ketan Patil

Ketki Gandhe

Kirti Khopkar

Manasi Surve

Manuel Teran

Meghna Kedia

Melonia Mendonca

Namesh Kher

Neeraja Ganesan

Neha Khedekar

Nidhi Chhajer

Nikhil Khekade

Nikhil Nambiar

Nina Sevilla

Nitin Patankar

Padma Shekar

Pankaj Rananavare

Pooja Chitrakar

Prasad Krishnan

Prashant Hegde

Prashant Hari

Pratik Malpe

Raghuvansh Ramaswamy

Rahul Goswami

Reema Rawtani

Reneta Jenik

Robert Huang

Rohit Bhangale
Ryan Everett
Saagar Chugh
Sandeep Khedekar
Shama Rangnekar
Shankar Krishnamurthy
Shashank Iyer
Shashank Kava
Shilpa Sreekrishnan
Shini Arora
Shraddha Ravishankar
Shrilata Murthy
Shrushti Parikh
Shruthi Ramakrishnan
Shruti Gupta
Shubalakshmi Shekar
Siddharth Deekshit
Siddharth Natarajan
Siddhi Pathak
Sneha Kantak

Sneha Solanki
Soham Mehta
Soumya Rajesh
Srinivasan Radhakrishnan
Sriram Bala
Sukanya Moorthy
Swati N Pevekar
Swati Nilesh Shahdadpuri
Tanay Shah
Utkarsha Prakash
Uzma Tafsir
Venkatakrisnaa Rajagopalan
Venkatesh Veeraraghavan
Vidya Iyer
Vikesh Chauhan
Vishal Pareek
Vivek Anandaramu
Yamini Menon
Yashaswi Kumar
Yugandhar Garde

APPENDIX

INTRODUCTION

Caldwell, Austin. "67 Ecommerce Stats and Facts to Know in 2021." Netsuite. April 15, 2021. https://www.netsuite.com/portal/resource/articles/ecommerce/ecommerce-statistics.shtml.

Research and Markets. "Global Online Education Market—Forecasts From 2020 To 2025." Accessed October 13, 2021. https://www.researchandmarkets.com/reports/4986759/global-online-education-market-forecasts-from.

Tricot, Roland. "Venture Capital Investments in Artificial Intelligence." OECD iLibrary. September 30, 2021. https://www.oecd-ilibrary.org/science-and-technology/venture-capital-investments-in-artificial-intelligence_f97beae7-en;jsessionid=19xwphvOPDUEQ5aR1HqCuHCH.ip-10-240-5-17.

CHAPTER 1—THE STARTUP MINDSET

Business Insider. "Jeff Bezos Talks Amazon, Blue Origin, Family, and Wealth." May 5, 2018. Video, 48:30. https://www.youtube.com/watch?v=SCpgKvZB_VQ&t-=719s&ab_channel=BusinessInsider.

FAQs. "What Do You Look for in a Founding Team?" Accessed October 15, 2021. First Round Capital. https://firstround.com/.

CHAPTER 2—THE STARTUP IDEATION

Princeton University. "Amazon Founder Jeff Bezos Delivers Princeton University's 2010 Baccalaureate Address." August 27, 2010. 18:43. https://www.youtube.com/watch?v=Duml1SHJqNE&ab_channel=PrincetonUniversity.

Richter, Felix. "Amazon Leads $150-Billion Cloud Market." Statista. July 5, 2021. https://www.statista.com/chart/18819/worldwide-market-share-of-leading-cloud-infrastructure-service-providers/.

TED. "The Single Biggest Reason Why Start-ups Succeed | Bill Gross." June 1, 2015. 6:40. https://youtu.be/bNpx7gpSqbY.

Y Combinator. "The Biggest Mistakes First-Time Founders Make—Michael Seibel." August 16, 2019. 7:03. https://youtu.be/D56QeyyQMLI.

CHAPTER 3—THE STARTUP BUSINESS MODEL

Armstrong, Stephen. "The untold story of Stripe, the secretive $20bn startup driving Apple, Amazon, and Facebook." WIRED. May 10, 2018. https://www.wired.co.uk/article/stripe-payments-apple-amazon-facebook.

Magretta, Joan. "Why Business Models Matter." Harvard Business Review. May 2002. https://hbr.org/2002/05/why-business-models-matter.

Ovans, Andrea. "What Is a Business Model?" Harvard Business Review. January 23, 2015. https://hbr.org/2015/01/what-is-a-business-model.

Strategyzer. "From Idea to Business—Animated Series." Last updated on July 2, 2014. https://youtube.com/playlist?list=PLBh9hoLWoawphbpU-vC1DofjagNqG1Qdf3.

CHAPTER 4—THE STARTUP COFOUNDER

Ghosh, Shikar, and Marilyn Morgan Westner. Contributors—Matt Fischer. "Key Terms to Include in a Founders' Agreement." Harvard Business School Accelerate. Date accessed—October 15, 2021. https://www.hbsaccelerate.org/people/founding-team/key-terms-to-include-in-a-founders-agreement/.

Ghosh, Shikar, and Marilyn Morgan Westner. Contributors—Matt Fischer, Lara O'Connor Hodgson, Rajesh Yabaji. "Co-Founder Equity Splits—Ways to Approach Allocations." Harvard Business School Accelerate. Date accessed—October 15, 2021. https://www.hbsaccelerate.org/people/founding-team/co-founder-equity-splits-ways-to-approach-allocations/.

Taggar, Harj. "How to Find the Right Co-Founder." Y Combinator. Date accessed—October 15, 2021. https://www.ycombinator.com/library/8h-how-to-find-the-right-co-founder.

Teare, Gené. "Sole Female Founders Raised $1B Less In 2020 Despite Record Venture Funding Surge In the US." Crunchbase News. March 24, 2021. https://news.crunchbase.com/news/sole-female-founders-raised-1b-less-in-2020-despite-record-venture-funding-surge-in-the-us/.

CHAPTER 5—THE STARTUP EXECUTION—PHASE ONE

DropDaBox. "Dropbox Intro Video." November 16, 2009. 2:16. https://www.youtube.com/watch?v=w4eTR7tci6A&ab_channel=DropDaBox.

Ries, Eric. "How Dropbox Started as a Minimal Viable Product." Tech Crunch. October 19, 2011. https://techcrunch.com/2011/10/19/dropbox-minimal-viable-product/.

CHAPTER 6—THE STARTUP EVOLUTION—THE ROAD TO PRODUCT/MARKET FIT

Blystone, Dan. "The Story of Instagram: The Rise of the #1 Photo-Sharing Application." Investopedia. June 06, 2020. https://www.investopedia.com/articles/investing/102615/story-instagram-rise-1-photoosharing-app.asp.

Brown, Brené. "Brené with Eric Mosley on Making Work Human." November 23, 2020. https://brenebrown.com/podcast/brene-with-eric-mosley-on-making-work-human/.

Fuchs, Jay. "When, Why, & How to Pivot a Startup Business." Hubspot. Accessed October 15, 2021. https://blog.hubspot.com/sales/pivot-startup.

Kirtley, Jacqueline and O'Mahony, Siobhan. What is a Pivot? Explaining When and How Entrepreneurial Firms Decide to Make Strategic Change and Pivot. Stanford SIEPR. September 20, 2018. https://siepr.stanford.edu/system/files/WhatIsAPivot_KirtleyOMahony_09202018.pdf

Popper, Ben. "Justin.tv, the Live Video Pioneer that Birthed Twitch, Officially Shuts Down." August 5, 2014. https://www.theverge.com/2014/8/5/5971939/justin-tv-the-live-video-pioneer-that-birthed-twitch-officially-shuts.

Saxena, Prateek. "An Entrepreneur's Guide to Successfully Pivot Your Startup." Appinventiv. July 10, 2020. https://appinventiv.com/blog/startup-pivot-guide/.

Shah, Hiten. "How Slack Became a $16 Billion Business by Making Work Less Boring." Nira blog. Date accessed—October 15, 2021.
https://nira.com/slack-history/.

Shontell, Alyson. "Twitch CEO: Here's Why We Sold to Amazon For $970 Million." August 25, 2014.
https://www.businessinsider.com/twitch-ceo-heres-why-we-sold-to-amazon-for-970-million-2014-8.

CHAPTER 7—THE STARTUP JAZZ

Aziz, Afdhel. "The Power of Purpose: The Business Case for Purpose (All the Data You Were Looking for Pt 1)." Forbes. May 7, 2020.
https://www.forbes.com/sites/afdhelaziz/2020/03/07/the-power-of-purpose-the-business-case-for-purpose-all-the-data-you-were-looking-for-pt-1/?sh=4044054d30ba.

Bright Girls Company. "Green Toys; From Her Playroom to Millions of Yours." March 10, 2015. Date Accessed—October 20, 2021.
https://brightgirlscompany.com/2015/03/green-toys-from-her-playroom-to-millions-of-yours/.

CBInsights. "The Complete List of Unicorn Companies." Last modified October 2021.
https://www.cbinsights.com/research-unicorn-companies.

Cone/Porter Novelli. "2018 Cone/Porter Novelli Purpose Study: How to Build Deeper Bonds, Amplify Your Message and Expand the Consumer Base." 2018. https://www.conecomm.com/research-blog/2018-purpose-study.

Dewez, Alexandre. "Voodoo Games Deep Dive—Another French Unicorn Is Born." Overlooked #32. August 27, 2020. https://alexandre.substack.com/p/-voodoo-games-another-french-unicorn.

Gibbon, Kevin. "I Can't Wait for You to See What We Do Next." LinkedIn. March 27, 2018. https://www.linkedin.com/pulse/i-cant-wait-you-see-what-we-do-next-kevin-gibbon/.

Glassdoor. "Working at Bumble." Date Accessed—November 17, 2021. https://www.glassdoor.com/Overview/Working-at-Bumble-EI_IE1161959.11,17.htm.

Green Toys. "How We Make 100% Recycled Toys." Date Accessed—October 20, 2021. https://www.greentoys.com/pages/our-story.

IBM Newsroom. "IBM Study: Purpose and Provenance Drive Bigger Profits for Consumer Goods in 2020." January 10, 2020. https://newsroom.ibm.com/2020-01-10-IBM-Study-Purpose-and-Provenance-Drive-Bigger-Profits-for-Consumer-Goods-In-2020.

McCracken, Harry. "How Shyp Sunk: The Rise and Fall of an On-Demand Startup." Fast Company. March 27. 2018. https://www.fastcompany.com/40549442/how-shyp-sunk-the-rise-and-fall-of-an-on-demand-startup.

PandoDaily. "PandoMonthly: Fireside Chat with Airbnb CEO Brian Chesky." January 14, 2013. 3:01:53. https://youtu.be/6yPfxcqEXhE.

Sairam, Erin Spencer. "Women Thrive At The Bumble Hive." Forbes. July 3, 2018. https://www.forbes.com/sites/erinspencer1/2018/07/03/women-thrive-at-the-bumble-hive/?sh=12f8ca875741.

CHAPTER 8—THE STARTUP MEASUREMENTS

Bercovici, Jeff. "How This Millennial Founder Created a $730 Million Fashion Startup—With the Help of an Algorithm. Proving that data-powered humans really can build a better fashion retail business." Inc. Magazine. October 2017. https://www.inc.com/magazine/201710/jeff-bercovici/stitch-fix-katrina-lake.html.

Goodwater Thesis. "Understanding Stitch Fix: Finding the Perfect Fit." Goodwater. November 13, 2017. https://www.goodwatercap.com/thesis/understanding-stitch-fix.

Pressler, Jessica. "How Stitch Fix's CEO Katrina Lake Built A $2 Billion Company." Elle magazine. February 28, 2018. https://www.elle.com/fashion/a15895336/katrina-lake-stitch-fix-ceo-interview/.

CHAPTER 9—THE STARTUP TEAM

Alkurd, Ibrahim. "Five Strategies for Retaining Employees."
Forbes. September 25, 2020.
https://www.forbes.com/sites/theyec/2020/09/25/five-strate-
gies-for-retaining-employees/?sh=6128969678b7.

Hower, Lewis. "Deciding How Much Equity to Give to Your Key
Employees." January 9, 2020.
https://www.forbes.com/sites/theyec/2020/09/25/five-strate-
gies-for-retaining-employees/?sh=6128969678b7.

CHAPTER 10—THE STARTUP MARKETING

Livemint. "*The Souled Store Raises ₹75 Crore from Elevation
Capital.*" *Updated: 04 Aug 2021.*
*https://www.livemint.com/companies/start-ups/the-souled-
store-raises-rs-75-crore-from-elevation-capital-11628060126364.
html.*

Optimizely. "Search Engine Marketing." Accessed October 15,
2021.
https://www.optimizely.com/optimization-glossary/
search-engine-marketing/.

Slidebean. "How We Made $2.5MM from YouTube and Google."
May 26, 2020. 10:58.
https://youtu.be/_3_aAxneu2w.

Statista. "Social Media Advertising Spending in the United
States from 2019 to 2021." January 2021.
https://www.statista.com/statistics/246341/social-media-ad-
vertising-spending-in-the-us/.

Weinberg, Gabriel and Justin Mares. "Traction: How Any Startup Can Achieve Explosive Customer Growth." Penguin Books Limited. October 6, 2015.

CHAPTER 11—THE STARTUP NETWORK—INVESTORS, ADVISORS, AND ACCELERATORS

First Round. FAQs. Accessed October 15, 2021. https://firstround.com/.

Fundz. "Series A, B, C Funding: Averages, Investors, Valuations." https://www.fundz.net/what-is-series-a-funding-series-b-funding-and-more.

Jurkovskaja, Roxane. "5 Things to Consider Before Joining an Accelerator." Startup Grind. https://www.startupgrind.com/blog/5-things-to-consider-before-joining-an-accelerator/.

Morill, Danielle. "Top 3 Startup Accelerators Produce Nearly 10% of U.S. Series A Deals." Matterkmark. January 9, 2017. https://mattermark.com/top-3-startup-accelerators-produce-series-a/.

Reiff, Nathan. "Series A, B, C Funding: How It Works." Investopedia. May 31, 2021. https://www.investopedia.com/articles/personal-finance/102015/series-b-c-funding-what-it-all-means-and-how-it-works.asp.

Sridharan. Karthik. "6 Pros and Cons of Joining a Startup Accelerator." Wharton Magazine. February 25, 2016.

https://magazine.wharton.upenn.edu/digital/6-pros-and-cons-of-joining-a-startup-accelerator/

CHAPTER 13—THE STARTUP FAILURE—HOW TO SURVIVE REJECTION

Steve Next. "Steve Jobs 1995 Interview NeXT Computer." Vimeo. November 8, 2011. https://vimeo.com/31813340.

CONCLUSION

Embroker. "106 Must-Know Startup Statistics for 2021." September 30, 2021. https://www.embroker.com/blog/startup-statistics/.